THE BEGINNER'S G[U]

HUNTING DEER FOR FOOD

JACKSON LANDERS

Storey Publishing

The mission of Storey Publishing is to serve our customers by
publishing practical information that encourages
personal independence in harmony with the environment.

Edited by Carleen Madigan
Art direction and book design by Alethea Morrison
Text production by Liseann Karandisecky

Cover illustration by © William Howell Golson
Interior illustrations by © Robert Smith

Indexed by Christine R. Lindemer, Boston Road Communications

Storey Publishing
210 MASS MoCA Way
North Adams, MA 01247
www.storey.com

Printed in the United States by Malloy Incorporated
10 9 8 7 6 5 4 3 2 1

Library of Congress Cataloging-in-Publication Data

Landers, Jackson.
 The beginner's guide to hunting deer for food / by Jackson Landers.
    p. cm.
  Includes index.
  ISBN 978-1-60342-728-9 (pbk. : alk. paper)
  1. Deer hunting. 2. Venison. I. Title.
SK301.L292 2011
799.2'765—dc22

2011010314

CONTENTS

AN INTRODUCTION TO HUNTING............5

CHAPTER 1 **UNDERSTANDING DEER** 15

CHAPTER 2 **WHITETAIL ANATOMY AND BIOLOGY** 26

CHAPTER 3 **THE EVOLUTION OF DEER** 37

CHAPTER 4 **CHOOSE YOUR WEAPON** 47

CHAPTER 5 **TACTICS** 90

CHAPTER 6 **SHOT PLACEMENT** 109

CHAPTER 7 **AFTER THE SHOT** 120

CHAPTER 8 **OKAY, IT'S DOWN: NOW WHAT?** 130

CHAPTER 9 **BUTCHERING** 141

CHAPTER 10 **COOKING** 154

CHAPTER 11 **WHERE TO HUNT** 166

RESOURCES........................... 172

INDEX 173

Acknowledgments

My gratitude goes to Erin Bauer, without whom I never would have started to write a book. Also to Jenny McLellan Doskey, who got me over the hump. Finally to my wife, Tricia Smith, for her help all along the way, especially with the recipes.

AN INTRODUCTION TO HUNTING

You probably wouldn't be holding this book right now if you didn't intend to eat meat. There is a story behind every bite of chicken, beef, or venison, and that story began somewhere with a living creature. We should consider what that story is when we choose what we are going to eat.

We can buy factory-farmed meat at any grocery store and accept whatever were the hormones, antibiotics, diet, and living conditions that produced the most meat for the least amount of money. Or we can get fussier about the labels and seek out something that is certified as organic or grass-fed or free range. Perhaps there is a local farmer or rancher to purchase meat from directly. If you have enough land, you might even try raising your own livestock for food.

Yet there is another ready source of meat available to most people in North America. We can learn how to hunt for it in the wild or in some cases in our own backyards. Meat doesn't get much more free range than that. For the cost of some basic equipment (some of which can last a lifetime) and a little bit of education, it is possible to stop paying directly for meat altogether while eating no less of it.

The meat hunter does not need to make sense of any labels. Every deer that he or she eats is, without question, both free range and locally produced. That wild animal has almost certainly not been injected with any antibiotics or hormones. As far as humane treatment is concerned, the experience of the animal is in your hands.

I will not sugarcoat the fact that hunting means killing. When we think about hunting, our minds go straight to the kill, and we are forced to confront the inherent brutality of it. The idea of farming or ranching provides an array of other images to distract us: contented cattle standing around in a field, munching on hay. Perhaps we recall a drive through the country as children, window rolled down, face into the wind, mooing loudly at the bored cows. The pastoral imagery gives us a mental dodge around the killing; we aren't able to do that with hunting. But make no mistake: farmed cattle or chickens are killed just as surely and as violently as a hunted deer. Shrink-wrapped packages of prebutchered meat at the grocery store make it easy to ignore what it is all really about. Many of us recoil slightly at the sight of pigs' feet on display beside the pork chops, not because there is anything wrong with them as food, but because the sight of an actual severed foot demands that we confront what meat really is.

There are millions of us who feel bad about eating meat — but not bad enough to actually stop doing it. Hunting for some or all of our own meat can be a good compromise. Hunting for food is, ethically speaking, the next best thing to being a vegetarian.

Why Hunt?

There are other very sound reasons why more people should take up hunting as an alternative to purchasing commercially raised food. Hunting can be a very good way of reducing the consumption of fossil fuels in your own life. Many people have now become aware of the concept of "food miles," thanks to such writers as Michael Pollan. The term *food miles* describes the distance that your food and its components had to travel to reach your plate. For example, a tomato eaten in New York

City in December certainly isn't very local. It may have been grown in California before being packed and shipped across the country; that's at least 3,000 food miles right there. Gasoline and diesel are what moved it to someone's plate, with the attendant pollution and carbon dioxide emissions. Then figure in the petroleum used for fertilizer and the manufacturing of any packaging. The environmental impact adds up.

EATING LOCALLY

Hunting for deer is an opportunity to measure the carbon footprint of your food simply by checking your odometer on the way home from a hunt. In my own case, most of my venison is harvested literally in my own backyard and butchered in my own kitchen. Food miles = 0. I suppose you might count the carbon dioxide that I exhaled while carrying the quarters of meat into the house.

If you live in the United States, odds are that there are wild deer within 10 miles of wherever you are sitting right now. If you happen to be on the East Coast, there could very well be one in your backyard. Food doesn't get any more local than that.

EATING WELL

In many ways, deer meat is better for you than beef is. Venison contains far less fat than beef does, and while deer do put on fat, it is not marbled within the meat, the way beef fat is. Most of the fat tends to be right under the skin and is removed completely during the butchering process.

Wild venison is also as natural as meat can get. It hasn't been injected with antibiotics or hormones. It is possible to buy "organic" meat that has been subjected to a minimum of this kind of interference, but since the introduction of loose (rather than strict) federal standards, we have seen the practical definition of *organic* stretched to the point of absurdity and irrelevance.

UTILIZING NATURAL RESOURCES TO SAVE MONEY

Deer represent a means of converting land with other primary uses into a dual-use area that produces food. An area of mixed fields and forests bordering on a suburban housing development is providing natural habitat for many wild animals, housing for human beings, and recreational areas in the backyards. In the eastern United States, it is also probably producing about 8 pounds of edible venison per acre, per year. Yet most of that food is going to waste, eventually rotting by the side of the road after collisions with cars.

A typical deer harvested in my own area of central Virginia weighs around 100 pounds. After you subtract the weight of the digestive system, skeleton, respiratory system, hide, and various other inedibles (some of these organs can be eaten if you really want to), you can expect to harvest around 40 pounds of meat. When compared with beef at the grocery store, averaging around $7 per pound among the various cuts, that one deer represents $280 worth of groceries. Like much of North America, my home state of Virginia offers liberal bag limits on a basic license, because of the high numbers of deer. A hunter who takes the maximum of six deer on a basic license can end up with as much as $1,680 worth of food in the freezer every year.

You probably won't get this kind of bang for your buck out of planting a vegetable garden. And hunting requires much less work — you don't have to weed, fertilize, or water a deer. Consider how much vegetable gardening and deer hunting have in common. Both are methods of converting nutrients in the local soil into an edible form for your consumption. Both are means of reducing your total food miles and taking control of your diet at the very source. The difference is that a hunter lets the deer do the busywork all year and also gets the consumptive benefit of the (essentially borrowed) land the deer was grazing on.

Why Hunt *Deer?*

There are other nonendangered animals you can hunt in North America, such as squirrels, rabbits, and turkeys, but the total weight of meat to be had from these animals following a successful day of hunting is very small compared to that of the meat from a single deer.

Animals of a size similar to deer are around, but not in the same densities as deer. In some parts of the country, black bears are quite common, but they are extremely difficult to hunt without using bait. Bait for bears is illegal in many parts of the country, and annual bag limits are usually a single bear. So specializing in hunting bears for food would not make sense for very many people. Pronghorn antelope seem like a good option in some parts of America, but bag limits on these animals tend to be low in western states, and hunting them is more of a physical challenge than hunting whitetail deer. Elk are an option in some places, but you may have to apply for a special permit or tag to hunt elk in your state, and butchering an animal that can weigh 400 to 1,000 pounds is a bit more work than is butchering a typical deer.

When all is said and done, whitetail deer represent a uniquely ideal opportunity for the locavore hunter, in terms of time and effort measured against the yield of food. If you are going to pick one type of prey to specialize in hunting, whitetail deer and their close relatives (including blacktails and mule deer) are the logical choice in most of North America.

Learning to Hunt as an Adult

Many of us who are concerned about such issues as animal cruelty, healthy diets, CO_2 emissions, and local food did not grow up in hunting or shooting households. Most people learned to hunt by growing up with a family member who hunted; they apprenticed as children and teenagers and never really had to think about learning *how* to hunt for their food. People are less inclined to take up hunting as adults because they lack the opportunity and knowledge needed to get started.

There are two major hurdles for the adult novice to overcome. The first is acquiring the knowledge necessary to be a safe and successful hunter. You can find most of that within the pages of this book. The second hurdle is facing the brutal reality of where meat comes from. It's one thing to remove the shrink-wrap from a precut steak and dip it in some marinade; it is quite another matter to kneel, alone, beside the warm, still body of a large animal in the frozen morning air with a knife in your hand, contemplating how you're going to turn this beast into food.

Don't Skip Hunter's Education

EVERY STATE in the United States has some type of public program to teach new hunters how to hunt safely and legally. This book is not intended to be a substitute for such a class.

Most states require that a hunter take and pass a hunter's education class before receiving a hunting license.

A typical hunter's ed class will teach you:

- How to understand the seasons and bag limits for wild game in your area
- How to safely load and carry a firearm while hunting
- The legal responsibilities of a hunter before and after a kill
- When not to pull the trigger
- What types of weapons and tactics are legal in your area
- Where you are and are not permitted to hunt

PSYCHOLOGICAL PREPARATION

Hunters in this country are frequently stereotyped and vilified. We are usually depicted in film and television as either bumbling fools in red mackinaws and hats with silly earflaps or pathologically bloodthirsty murderers who despise animals. We are supposed to be either stupid or cruel, and the well-meaning makers of such movies as *Open Season* can never seem to fathom the possibility that someone might hunt for rational reasons.

The central question about the sanity of hunters is arguably how we feel about the kill. There has been plenty of good psychological research on hunters that demonstrates that they are not bloodthirsty. But none of us can really vouch 100 percent for what is going on in the mind of anyone except ourselves, so I will describe what I have found to be the emotional experience of the culmination of a hunt.

From the moment I first see a deer within range, my emotional state is one of hope, anticipation, and focus. I have never felt a sensation of hatred or aggression toward the animal. I go through a mental checklist in the space of what is probably a fraction of a second, considering whether the shot is both practical and safe.

Surprisingly, despite the fact that I am about to unleash this deadly force against a living creature, the act of taking the shot does not feel violent to me at the time. For reasons that I cannot explain, I usually do not hear the sound of the gunshot from the rifle that is right in front of my face. What I do often hear is the silence that immediately follows as every bird and squirrel in the forest stops in its tracks. Unconsciously, I work the bolt of the rifle, ejecting the brass casing and chambering a fresh cartridge in case a follow-up shot is needed. I smell the gun smoke that drifts out of the chamber when I open it. Time slows down.

Afterward, I approach the deer. The sensation of seeing it up close and touching its warm body is not unlike experiences I have had in cracking open pieces of shale and finding perfect imprints of Carboniferous ferns. Here is a living thing in all its minute perfection that no human has ever examined before. Here are tidy black hooves with surprisingly soft bottoms that no person has ever touched before. Here is a sleek belly with an L-shaped scar on it that nobody would ever have known existed.

No matter how many fossils I find or how many deer I kill, that sense of overwhelming awe will never fade away.

Next comes the sadness at the fact that the deer is dead. I am reasonably certain that deer are self-aware, and they certainly feel pain. I do not know what happens to the ego of the deer after I have killed it. It was a unique, self-aware consciousness that had a set of experiences and a way of looking at the world, and now that thing is gone. Does it dissolve? Or is it hovering over me at that very moment, watching me kneel beside its dead body? I have no idea, but there is no escaping the contemplation of that question. The possibility that the deer is witnessing everything leads me to treat it with a particular reverence.

Finally, I experience relief and gratitude. I hunt for food, after all. Money is often tight, and I have a family to feed. When there is no money for groceries and I have no idea what we are going to eat for dinner the next night, the sense of relief at having secured 40 pounds of meat is tremendous. Knowing that I will not be walking back to the house empty-handed after sundown is a very good feeling.

Is it psychopathic to become comfortable with killing for food? I really don't think so. Predation is so fundamental to nature that it seems absurd to demonize it for any animal, including humans.

When I consider myself before and then after I took up hunting, I can honestly say that it has improved me. Hunting for food has given me an increased reverence for life by virtue of my having to confront directly the unsanitized reality of an animal's death. I can't look at packaged meat in the grocery store the same way I once did. I am not arguing that this change of perspective in itself justifies the act of killing, but it is an essential point in the consideration of a hunter's psychology.

I think that anyone who is considering taking up deer hunting for the first time will feel some amount of trepidation regarding the actual kill. Some would-be hunters admit as much freely; others brashly dismiss deer as overgrown rats and convey a sort of artificial glee at the thought of exterminating them. I have seen far more of the latter behavior from nonhunters than I have from people who have actually hunted and killed deer. You may say that you hate deer because you have to chase them away from your hostas all summer, but your opinion would probably be tempered after coming face to face with a dying animal.

In my experience, the best way to be emotionally prepared for the act of killing a deer is to be hungry and broke when you are hunting. A big part of the reason I became a dedicated deer hunter was lack of money for groceries. Having a real need to feed your family will erase any doubts about what you are doing. The deer dies so that you and the people you are feeding can live. This has been the essence of predation since time immemorial. It is utterly rational, natural, and, I think, moral.

Once the deer is down, one thing is certain. No matter what else goes wrong in your life — if the car breaks down or you lose your job or the furnace breaks — you will not starve. Everything else might go all to hell, but you have the food department covered for the next month. Someone who has been wealthy for his entire life may have difficulty really grasping this. Anyone who has ever unwillingly gone to bed hungry, especially someone with children, will find that any guilt over killing is dwarfed by the relief of knowing that much meat is going into the fridge.

THE FIRST TIME I KILLED A DEER on a hunt I was 29 years old. It was a cool, clear autumn afternoon. I'd left work a few hours early in hopes of seeing a deer in the meadow beside my house. Before hunting, I had to go into the house to check on my dog, Simon.

Simon, a German shepherd mix, was paralyzed from the neck down. He had a pair of herniated disks in his neck that had swelled enough to pinch his spinal cord, preventing any movement of his limbs. Surgery was an option, but I didn't have the money. People shook their heads at me and told me to "put him down." Weeks had passed like this. I nursed him, hoping that he would recover. When an animal is ready to die, I find that it will manage to let you know one way or another. Simon wasn't ready to quit.

As I came inside, he woofed and thumped his black-and-tan tail a few times, the only motion below the neck that he was capable of. We spent a few minutes together. I gave him some water, then shouldered my rifle and left him on a dog bed in the kitchen.

I sat on a stool at the edge of the long meadow of sun-bleached, waist-high grass. The grass served to hide me as long as I stayed low. There was a faint odor of wood smoke. Because of the slope of the ground and the height of the grass, I could see what was 50 yards away from me but not what was only 5 or 10 yards away.

After about 5 minutes, I had the most absurd feeling that I should stand up. I cannot recommend this to anyone, since logically it should serve only to expose the hunter to any prey. But I stood up anyhow, and when I did I saw that there was a deer standing a few yards in front of me. The deer had no antlers. It looked straight at me, unmoving, as I shouldered my rifle. I looked at it through the crosshairs of the scope, taking care to center it over the lungs. I took a quick, deep breath. Slowly, I exhaled and near the bottom of the breath I squeezed the trigger.

The deer collapsed. It was as if the animal had an "off" switch that had been pulled. I did not hear the sound of a shot, though there must have been one. Reflexively, I worked the bolt of my rifle in order to eject the empty case and chamber a new one. With the rifle still at my shoulder, I stepped slowly toward the deer.

continued on next page

It was a button buck, a male deer without a proper set of antlers. It was dead. I laid down my rifle, knelt down, and touched its sleek gray body and white belly. I saw many little details that I had never known existed on a deer's body. The hooves, both hard and soft at the same time. Bloated, beige ticks clung to the edges of the stiff ears. The bullet hole was a few inches higher than I had intended. I could see that it must have gone through the tops of the lungs as well as clipped through the spine (this was confirmed during butchering).

Somehow I was going to have to gut this thing. I unloaded the rifle and walked back to the house to fetch a few tools. When I walked inside, I could see down the hallway that Simon was not where I had left him. I found him in the bathroom, facing the corner between the toilet and the bathtub. This was the same place that Simon always used to run to when he heard the sound of thunder or any loud noise resembling thunder . . . like a gunshot.

The realization quickly dawned that Simon must have gotten up on his own legs and scrambled into the bathroom at the sound of my shot on the deer. His spinal injury was miraculously cured at the precise instant that the deer's spine was severed by the bullet.

In spite of the blood and the mess and the total confusion as to how to go about the job, there was never a happier man who found himself gutting a deer. Simon walked out of the house and ran back in on his own legs. He was completely exhausted by the effort, but he had walked all the same. This marked the start of what proved to be a total recovery. I dragged the gutted deer to the concrete front walk of my rural home and quartered it, with Simon on the grass beside me. I carved off rich, red strips of raw meat and fed them to him as I worked.

I was grateful to the deer that I killed. At the time, I had very little money for groceries, and we needed the meat badly. My gratitude increased tenfold after I realized that Simon had been cured. What I never felt that day was guilt. Having just witnessed a miracle set into motion by my shot at the deer, it was in fact the happiest day of my life thus far. Magic and miracle volunteered to intertwine themselves into my hunt, and since that time they have never really left.

CHAPTER ONE

UNDERSTANDING DEER

Having established that hunting deer is a useful pursuit for a locavore, our next question is how to actually *get* a deer. You'd think that this part would be easy. We see deer everywhere — in backyards, by the side of the road, along the runway at the airport. The trouble is that we aren't allowed to hunt in most of these places. The deer know they're safe in these places, which is why you see them there so often. The animals that are so easy to take for granted as something akin to overgrown mice are, in fact, considered by many experienced hunters to be among the world's most mentally challenging prey.

Teddy Roosevelt had this to say about the whitetail deer:

> *The whitetail deer is much the commonest game animal of the United
> States, being still found, though generally in greatly diminished
> numbers throughout most of the Union. It is a shrewd, wary, knowing
> beast; but it owes its prolonged stay in the land chiefly to the fact that
> it is an inveterate skulker, and fond of the thickest cover. Accordingly
> it usually has to be killed by stealth and stratagem, and not by fair,
> manly hunting.*

"Fair, manly hunting," in Roosevelt's eyes (as well as those of
most hunters during his time), consisted of chasing down wild animals
on horseback and other methods of hunting that were in some way
exhilarating and physically demanding. But it's telling to look at what
native animals survived that era of "fair, manly hunting." The native elk
and bison that were once common in the eastern states are long gone.
Bison will never fully recover, even out west or on the Great Plains. Whitetail deer remained and thrived because, among other things, they were so
very hard to kill.

Fair and manly, indeed.

Elk and bison are often hunted by finding some sign, such
as droppings or footprints, following it until the prey is within sight
(through whatever rough country the animal has traversed), then making
a careful shot. Elk hunts in particular are extremely physically demanding, but aren't rocket science. At the right time of year, it can be a matter
of sitting on a hilltop and "bugling" in a bull elk by simulating a mating
call. Elk and bison are big animals that usually have few predators to
worry about, so (as adults) they don't have much need to hide. This con-
trasts with the hunting of whitetails, which, owing to their habit of being,
as Teddy Roosevelt pointed out, "inveterate skulkers," requires a great
deal of thought and skill combined with a minimum of physical challenge. Whitetails do not just sneak and hide as a response to a specific,
immediate threat. They sneak around, sticking to cover and monitoring
good escape routes as a normal part of their day, whether or not they
have a reason to be afraid. Whitetail deer are the chess champs of the
hunting world.

Whitetail deer have been outrageously successful as a species in North America over the last 50 years in particular. They have thrived in the face of suburban sprawl and the industrialization of farming and ranching. Whitetails can live in eastern deciduous forests, suburban backyards, the Great Plains, and the sagebrush country of Texas. Whitetails are found in every U.S. state except Alaska. They range as far north as Saskatchewan and as far south as Peru. According to the U.S. Department of Agriculture's Wildlife Services Department, there are roughly 30 million deer in the United States alone. No animal can be this successful without being very well adapted to a life spent surrounded by human hunters and every other predator that has set foot in the Americas during the last few million years. The whitetail has outlasted the predation of terror birds, saber-toothed cats, the American cheetah, large tribes of hunter-gatherers, and now perhaps you.

A Year in the Life

To hunt whitetails, you need to understand them on a level that surpasses what is required to hunt most other wild animals. You can catch the "inveterate skulker" only by knowing what his motivations are and predicting his complex behavior. What is he eating at a given time of year? What is his mating behavior, and how does it change his daily habits? What are the limitations of his senses? An understanding of the animal's biology and natural history is essential. It is best to begin with an examination of a year in the life of the whitetail, starting with birth.

FAWNING SEASON

In my home state of Virginia, fawns are born during the month of May; this timing varies slightly in other latitudes. The coordination of pregnancy and birth among all members of the herd is something that deer have in common with most other hoofed mammals. Newborn and young deer are easy prey, but when the whole herd gives birth at once, the local predators are overwhelmed and cannot possibly find and eat a dangerous proportion of the fawns before the young deer have a chance to develop defensive behaviors.

A healthy doe will typically give birth to twins, occasionally triplets. Single births are most often associated with very young mothers, underfed deer, and elderly does. Siblings will not usually meet each other until around the sixth week of life. This is because of the habit whitetail does make of hiding their young in separate locations, which increases the odds that at least one of them will reach adulthood.

Though a whitetail fawn is technically capable of walking within an hour of birth, it cannot possibly keep up with its mother. A nursing doe has very high caloric demands: she is recovering from a winter during which she was living mostly off fat reserves from the previous fall, and she has to produce milk for several fawns. To cover sufficient ground to take in enough calories, she has to leave behind the fawns and return to nurse them about half a dozen times a day.

A fawn has very little scent. While even with our poorly developed sense of smell you or I can smell a mature whitetail from 50 yards downwind, a predator has to be within a yard or two to have even a chance of smelling a fawn. A fawn will sit very still all day while waiting for its mother to return. If it gets spooked and has to run a short distance for some reason, the doe finds it by making a quiet call, to which the fawn responds.

Predators — chiefly black bears and coyotes — account for a majority of fawn mortalities. But according to a study by the Pennsylvania Game Commission, the next most common cause of death for a fawn is, unfortunately, malnutrition. This starvation is the natural consequence of high deer population densities, which decrease the amount of quality forage available for nursing does (see Population Control and Malnutrition, facing page). When food is scarce, milk dries up, and it is the fawns that take the brunt of it.

Those fawns that are lucky enough to escape detection by bears and whose mothers are wise and enterprising enough to feed them adequately will usually be ready to start making limited rounds with their mothers by early July. They are beginning to eat some forage but are also still nursing. Even once their incisor teeth and premolars have come in, their digestive system needs to catch up.

WHEN THE TOP-LEVEL PREDATORS are removed from a habitat, herbivore numbers will increase at first. Eventually, though, they'll run out of food. Gray wolves and cougars, which were common predators of deer across most of North America a few hundred years ago, have been removed from most areas and are unlikely to return. Although black bears, coyotes, and bobcats will prey on fawns, they are only occasional predators of adult deer in most of their range. Human hunters are now the only animals that regularly prey on mature deer in most of North America.

It is easy to look at an area of deer habitat and get the impression that everything is fine. There are still plants growing, and the adult deer you see in the spring look a bit thin but are hardly skeletal. Contrary to what most gardeners probably think, however, deer do not eat every plant in the woods and fields. They need food with a high percentage of protein, but most of what is out there is just a lot of cellulose. Even when they can't find nourishing forage, deer keep eating — in fact, wildlife biologists have autopsied deer that have died of malnutrition and found bellies full of forage. It's the wrong kind of stuff, however, good for filling a stomach but not adequate for sustaining essential life functions.

A given area can support only a limited amount of biomass. When deer births continue at rates that evolved to keep pace with high predation, the result is the destruction of deer habitat and a population of animals that slowly starve to death. The human decision of whether to hunt them becomes a question of the death you see or the death you don't see.

Deer have a complex digestive system compared to that of humans. This system depends on a flourishing ecosystem of gastric bacteria, with various strains being more efficient than others at digesting different types of food. Even as adults, deer cannot move abruptly from one type of forage to another; it takes them a few days for the numbers of the required bacteria to get back up to full strength, as they gradually eat a little more of the new food every day. As fawns, they are still establishing these bacteria slowly and must continue to nurse, even while they are learning to eat forage.

Once the fawns are comfortable getting around and have learned to follow their mother's lead instantly, the doe will take her fawns to meet other does and fawns in the vicinity.

SPRING SOCIALIZING

Whitetails are essentially herd animals that are forced to disperse for part of the year because of a lack of concentrated food sources of the type that enable their distant relatives to remain in larger herds year-round. They form matriarchal groups with geographic ranges that form a sort of daisy-shaped Venn diagram (see below). The eldest doe will have the range in the center. Her daughters have adjoining ranges that overlap a bit, and their daughters have similarly overlapping ranges. This is, of course, typically interrupted in the real world by the presence of roads, steep slopes, or varying types of vegetation and cover that make one area better habitat for raising a fawn than another.

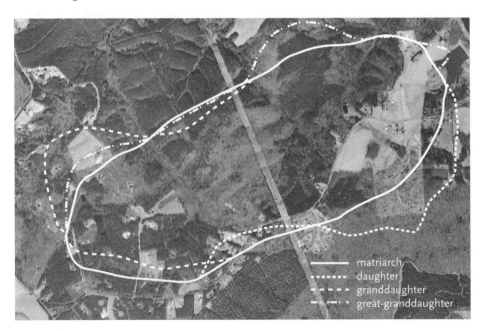

matriarch
daughter
granddaughter
great-granddaughter

Female whitetail deer stay in the same geographic area as their extended family.

Starting in late July, does begin to take their fawns around to socialize with the other does and fawns. This activity gradually increases, and by September bucks begin to join in the gatherings. The deer seek out large fields and meadows for these meetings, and you may see several dozen together at once. Close observation of their behavior will reveal that they are playing, sparring in a friendly way, and establishing where the new fawns are going to fit in the overall pecking order.

These friendly gatherings start to change in character gradually throughout September and October. By this time, the fawns have lost their spots and are completely weaned. By October they are no longer dependent on their mothers, although both doe and buck fawns will stay within this matriarchal system for 6 to 18 months.

THE RUT

Testosterone levels are increasing in the bodies of the bucks during this early-autumn period. Their bodies begin to change, and their necks swell. The friendly sparring gradually gives way to serious battles as does go into estrus, starting in late October. This marks the beginning of the annual highlight of the lives of whitetails, which is called *the rut*.

During the rut, bucks that have spent months grazing side by side will turn on each other. Buck fawns are often physically capable of mating, but their low social status makes it unlikely that they will do so, unless the population of mature bucks has been severely depleted by overharvest in previous years. Most buck fawns do not have proper antlers at this point. Rather, they have grown tiny nubs of bone on their heads. There are rare fawns that grow long spikes or even forked antlers, but most will be what are called *button bucks*.

"Button bucks" are buck fawns that are just starting to grow antlers.

The primary rut is sometimes highly concentrated in early November, with all deer in the area madly rushing around in search of mates and rivals. In other years, a rut may be more dispersed, with does going into estrus in a staggered fashion over the course of a month or so. There are many competing theories about what influences the start and coordination of the rut, but the dominant theory is that healthy does go into estrus in response to the phase of the moon. The rut tends to start earlier in southern latitudes and is poorly coordinated among deer living close to the equator.

Does and bucks behave differently during the rut. A doe will not typically compete with other does to mate with a buck, although if there is no buck available when she goes into estrus, she may travel far from her usual territory to find one. Bucks know that a doe is in estrus because her urine has a different scent, as do the chemicals produced by her scent glands. She may also make a vocalization known as an *estrous bleat*.

Even the most dominant among bucks is unlikely to breed more than five does each year. While whitetails are far from monogamous, a buck will tend to pair off with a single doe for about 3 days. They will travel and feed together, mating occasionally. The buck works to keep other bucks away from her until it is likely that she is pregnant with his offspring and she goes out of estrus.

In this sense, deer are not like cattle, where a single bull can breed an entire herd of cows. A minimum proportion of bucks to does is required to enable normal whitetail biology and society to function. With too few bucks, many does will not be bred during the rut and will go into heat again about a month later. This is usually referred to as the *rump rut*. Fawns that are conceived during a rump rut are born later in the spring and will have a lower weight going into the winter months of the next year. They are thus less likely to survive to maturity.

Doe fawns do not ordinarily participate in the rut, but between 5 and 20 percent of them (depending on which study you read) will go into heat during the rump rut. Doe fawns that become pregnant usually give birth to just a single fawn the following spring.

PREPARING FOR WINTER

When the rut is over, the deer are faced with the reality that they have been running around frantically for the last few weeks and have burned up most of their fat reserves. Fortunately, this is right around the time when most of the hard mast is dropping.

Hard mast refers to acorns, hickory nuts, beech nuts, and walnuts in a forest ecosystem. Deer devour acorns in great quantities. In different ecosystems, other plants may serve the same role. For example, in the Midwest, soybeans may be ripe and unharvested as late as the end of October. Whether it is through acorns or soybeans or another highly nutritious plant, the race is on to accumulate as much body fat as possible before the food is gone and the weather gets really cold.

By December, the fawns have reached their maximum skeletal size. The amounts of muscle and fat that hang from that skeleton may change from year to year, but if the fawn did not get enough to eat during its first 6 months, it will be permanently stunted.

In some areas, people are under the impression that the local deer are genetically predisposed toward small size when in fact they are under-size due to excessively high deer population densities compared to the available food. Here in my own county, in central Virginia, I have often observed that the mature deer in the southwestern portion of the county are only about two-thirds the size of those at the north end of the county. Yet in an area this small, it's practically impossible for any meaningful genetic isolation to be taking place; deer genes are constantly moving from one end of the county to the other. However, the quality of browse and hard mast, as well as the rate of hunting, can vary greatly in different parts of the county.

DISPERSAL

The vehicle by which these genes move from one area to another is primarily bucks that are in dispersal. At a point that can vary from 6 to 18 months of age, a buck fawn's mother will chase him away — not just out of her sight but actually out of his natal territory.

The evolutionary explanation for this is that forced dispersal prevents inbreeding. Doe fawns will ordinarily remain in or adjacent to their natal territory, where they can continue to socialize with their matriarchal group. But the young bucks that will eventually breed them will come from other, distant territories, up to 13 miles away (the mean distance is about 5 miles). Following this initial dispersal period, the vast majority of bucks will settle into core territories that will remain more or less constant for the rest of their lives.

Dispersal is unarguably the most dangerous time in a buck's life. The deer is forced to move into a new environment where it has no idea where the predators are, which roads are too busy to go near, and where the easier food sources are to be found. A great many of the killed deer that one finds by the side of the road are dispersal bucks. A buck fawn whose mother was killed during hunting season will not disperse but instead will remain in his natal territory. Because of this, buck fawns that are orphaned from October onward actually have a higher chance of survival than do buck fawns that are not orphaned.

SURVIVING WINTER

Winter is a tough time for whitetail deer. After the hard mast is gone, they graze on lawns and forest browse where they can find them. But overall, there's not a lot to eat. The size of the acorn drop in the fall has a significant impact on the rate of winter survival, particularly in colder climates. In Virginia our winters are usually mild enough that a deer going into winter without much fat is probably going to scrape by. But if there is a prolonged cold snap that requires burning extra calories to stay warm, that same deer may weaken and die before spring.

Usually, during February bucks shed their antlers. This is a good thing, because by that point antlers are often cracked or otherwise damaged by the fighting during the rut. Bucks have stopped being so rude to each other and have coalesced back into the small groups of two to six bucks, a situation that will persist until the next rut. This structure

When the rut has ended, bucks will seek out each other's company again. Their antlers may be cracked or broken from fighting and will soon drop off.

of buck society often disappears in populations where hunters disproportionately target bucks, whether through personal preference or archaic legal requirements that only antlered deer be hunted.

Bucks scrape and rub trees year-round, both during the rut and afterwards. There is a myth that scraping and rubbing is a territorial act intended to keep other bucks out of a territory, but the fact is that sociable groups of bucks have been observed rubbing their scent glands on the same thin sapling in full view of each other without any challenges or fights resulting. Scrapes and rubs appear to be a form of communication among deer.

SPRINGTIME

Bucks and does may settle back into different ranges as spring approaches, because of their differing requirements for nutrition and cover. A pregnant and soon-to-be-nursing doe needs food with a higher proportion of crude protein than a buck requires. She also needs plentiful cover within which to hide her fawns — not just one patch of cover that a bear or coyote will sniff out immediately, but so much cover that an animal searching for a fawn in it will be unlikely to find one. A buck needs a certain amount of protein, but he has less need for cover since he has fewer predators to be concerned about. This is not to say that bucks and does do not occupy the exact same habitat at times but simply that differing qualities of food and cover within a geographic area will tend to result in does and bucks favoring different territories.

By May, the bucks will begin to grow new antlers. At the peak of their growth, in July, they can often gain up to an inch of length each day, making antlers the fastest-growing tissue of any vertebrate.

This brings us full circle through a typical year in the life of a whitetail deer in Virginia. In this annual story of the life of a deer lie the keys to successfully hunting it. The hunting tactics that you may eventually learn or stumble upon will largely be exercises in exploiting the needs and motivations of the animal. Knowing the annual cycle of a deer is one part of this, and understanding how its body works is the other.

CHAPTER TWO

WHITETAIL ANATOMY AND BIOLOGY

The ability of the whitetail to thrive in nearly every part of North America is due in equal measure to its behavior and its physiology. There are a number of physical adaptations that allow the animal to eat the variety of foods that it does. Understanding how a deer's body works is the key to predicting much of its behavior. Becoming familiar with a deer's behavioral patterns and the reasons behind them is essential for successfully hunting it.

The Details of Deer Digestion

Depending on the time of year, deer consume a lot of browse. *Browse* refers to various types of leafy vegetation, such as herbaceous plants, the leaves of some deciduous trees, and the thinner green twigs and shoots of certain vines and shrubs. They snip this plant matter with the incisors of their lower jaw, which bear against a fleshy, textured pad on their top jaw (deer do not have any upper front teeth at all). The food may be chewed very briefly but is often swallowed more or less whole.

RUMINATING

Deer don't need to chew very much because they are ruminants — mammals belonging to the order Artiodactyla, which utilize a digestive organ called a rumen to digest their food in stages. This group of animals also includes cattle, camels, antelope, giraffes, and goats. When full, the rumen is easily the largest organ in the body of a deer (except for the epidermis).

When a deer eats, it swallows the food into the rumen, where it mixes with saliva. Saliva contains enzymes that break down cellulose and soften food. Various chambers within the rumen extract water and minerals from the food during this stage. The rumen is also filled with various types of bacteria that specialize in consuming and breaking down food that would have been indigestible otherwise.

At the deer's leisure, it regurgitates the food back into its mouth, where it uses its molars to chew the cud. After it has been chewed, the cud becomes more liquefied. When the deer swallows the cud again, it will settle out beneath the thicker, more recently chewed matter in the rumen. This allows the cud to pass into the deer's true stomach, which operates in a manner similar to that of the human stomach. Gastric acid breaks down some of the food into absorbable nutrients, and the food then continues through the small and large intestines, where the bacteria that consumed indigestible material back in the rumen are themselves digested. Finally, the undigested material is excreted.

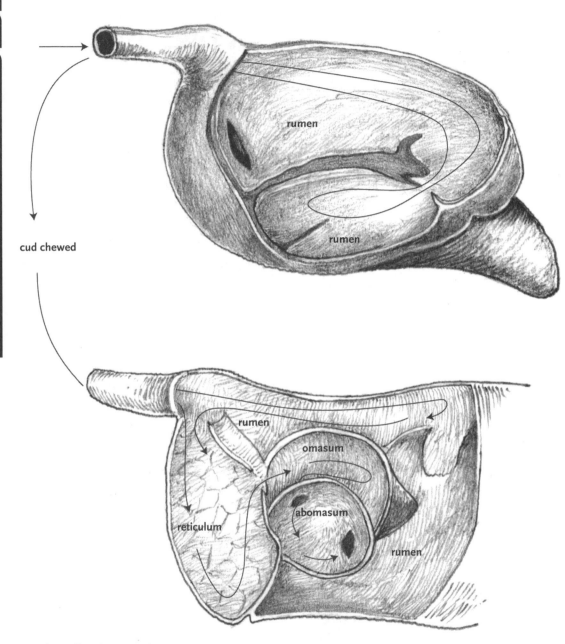

cud chewed

rumen

rumen

rumen

omasum

abomasum

reticulum

rumen

*A deer's digestive system has many
parts that enable it to digest a wide
variety of food.*

BENEFITS OF RUMINATING. This kind of digestive system offers several advantages to the deer. First, the symbiotic relationship with bacteria enables a deer to eat many foods that it could not otherwise make use of. If the deer cannot digest a plant directly, it gets bacteria to do the job, then digests the bacteria.

The other major advantage to ruminating is that deer can spend less time in the open while they're eating. If their digestive system was like ours, they would have to fully chew and swallow every bite while standing there in front of the food source. But deer don't really chew — they just grab food in their mouth and swallow it immediately. This way, they can hide in thick cover to do the chewing at their own pace.

Strategic Knowledge: Eating Patterns

THE DEER'S DEPENDENCE on different types of bacteria can be exploited tactically by a hunter.

A deer cannot abruptly switch from one food source to another — from acorns to browse, for example.

A deer needs to eat a little bit of browse at first to encourage an increase of the limited variety of bacteria that digest thin green twigs. It will take a few days for those microbes to multiply enough to handle a steady diet of the stuff.

For example, let's say that in mid-November there is a sudden storm that drops 8 inches of snow. The acorns are covered with snow, and it will take a lot of extra work on a deer's part to find them. What the deer would prefer to do is to switch to browse, assuming that any is present. A hunter should then expect to move to an area with good browse to ambush his or her prey. But don't move your hunting location for at least 2 days after the snow falls, because deer cannot make that transition right away. You'll find them pawing through the snow under the same oak trees where you found them the week before.

A rumen is also a sort of short-term food bank. If the weather is truly horrible for a day or if hunting pressure from predators is suddenly very intense, a deer can sit in the middle of a patch of briars for a day or two without getting hungry. This obviously can't last forever, but it gives the deer some flexibility in a crisis.

Eyesight

B ecause their eyes have adapted to seeing in the dark, deer are able to feed chiefly at night if they need to avoid predators, and will often "go nocturnal" in response to hunting pressure. Deer have a thin membrane, called a *tapetum lucidum,* that covers the back of the retina. It's a highly reflective bit of tissue that causes the shine of their eyes in the darkness that you've probably noticed when they're by the side of the road at night. The tapetum lucidum provides highly enhanced night vision, with the trade-off being that it also causes vision to be somewhat blurry at night. For example, on a night without much of a moon, humans would see mostly blackness and a few close objects in sharp detail. In the same conditions, an animal with a tapetum lucidum is likely to see the entire landscape, but with a little fuzziness around the edges.

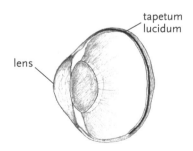

The tapetum lucidum enhances a deer's vision at night.

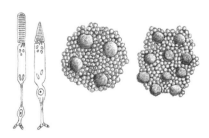

Rod and cone cells, named for their shape, are distributed across the retina in varying densities.

A deer's retinas also contain the same tiny rod and cone structures that ours do. Rods are very good at producing an image in dim conditions, but they perceive only light and dark. Cones are very good at distinguishing colors, but they require a lot more light to operate. There is only room for so many rods and so many cones; thus, any animal's vision is the product of a particular balance of rods and cones in a proportion that is most advantageous to the animal.

The process of evolution in deer has led to a greater proportion of rods to cones than human eyes have. The distribution of these structures within the retina is also different; consequently, deer do not see the same spectrum of color we do. The whole red end of the spectrum, including blaze orange, appears as shades of gray to them. But they do see the blue end of the spectrum quite well, extending even into the ultraviolet. Deer are more likely to notice someone in blue denim than they are someone wearing orange or red. This is doubly so because of the fact that, other than the sky, there is not much in the woods or fields that is naturally blue. Something large and blue is always worth paying attention to in a natural setting.

Because of their perception into the ultraviolet spectrum, deer can spot a modern human, even in camouflage clothing, more readily today than in the past. This is because of the various chemicals in modern laundry detergents that produce those "whiter whites." Even a dingy old white T-shirt washed with such a detergent will look brilliant to us in full sun. These UV brighteners produce a sort of glow that is more or less invisible to us in most light, but they cause clothing to stick out like a sore thumb to a deer.

These are details of deer vision that as hunters we need to be aware of. However, sight is not the primary way deer detect danger.

Hearing

There's a good reason that whitetail deer have those huge ears that swivel independently of their head — they give phenomenal hearing. I once sat hidden on a hillside, watching through a scope a deer that was more than 300 yards away, and flipped off the safety on my rifle. It was the tiniest metallic click. About a second later (just enough time for the sound to reach it), the deer looked up and swiveled its ears right at me.

Once a deer hears you or anything else in the woods, it will make one of three decisions. It might run away, far and fast. It could decide to investigate cautiously by making a wide circle around the source of the noise, in order to get downwind and pick up the scent of whatever is there. Or sometimes the deer will decide that you are noisy enough that it knows right where you are and can monitor the situation while continuing to feed. Of course, there are those once-in-a-blue-moon situations during the rut when a buck decides to charge straight at you. This is extremely rare, however.

When a deer, particularly a young one, has no other reason to feel jumpy, it may very well go with the third option, to stay put and not worry too much about the sound. The woods are full of noise throughout much of the day: there are other deer around; there are squirrels scurrying and rustling in the leaves; birds are foraging in the brush. If a deer took off every time it heard a sound, it would never be in one place long enough to satisfy its food needs.

Sense of Smell

Ears may be a deer's early-warning system, but a whitetail really tries to understand situations with its noses. Whitetails live in a world of scent. They communicate with each other using scent glands. They search for mates, identify food, and sniff out danger with their noses.

By wearing camouflage and staying very still, you might get away with having a deer looking straight at you and not realizing what you are. If you've attracted its attention by being noisy, you might be able to put it at ease by, say, imitating the sound of a squirrel chewing on a nut. But if a deer manages to catch your human scent, it will probably leave the area, unless it has become exceptionally habituated to the presence of humans. At all times, you must be conscious of the direction of the wind relative to you and to where deer are or might be.

However, you can sometimes turn the tables on a deer when it comes to tracking scent. Among the many scent glands on various parts of its body, a deer has *tarsal glands* on its legs that produce a scent indicating to other deer roughly what sex and age it is. The varied nuances of these scents and pheromones are lost on the human nose, but the basic funk is not. When downwind from a deer in the reasonably dry air of autumn and winter, you will be able to smell it when it's within 50 yards or so.

I once successfully found and killed a deer by using my nose in this manner. I was hunting around a 2-acre field of waist-high grass and brush. From past observation I knew that deer liked to use this as a bedding area during the middle of the day; it was perfect cover for deer to hide in. Slowly, I circled around the perimeter of the field, smelling the air every step of the way. When I came to the western side of the field, I caught the strong, almost horselike odor of a deer. I licked my finger and held it up to feel where the wind was. Then I faced into the wind and checked to make sure that there was no house or road nearby that my bullet might hit in a quick shot.

I lifted the rifle to my shoulder, lowered slightly so that I could look over the scope. I held my thumb on the safety, ready to flip it off, and advanced cautiously through the field. Suddenly, the deer stood up about 5 yards in front of me. I fired one shot, and it fell where it stood.

Antlers

M any sport hunters set their sights on bucks with big racks of antlers, but for a meat hunter like me, antlers aren't so important. If anything, does tend to be easier to hunt because so many other hunters are in the habit of targeting bucks. But there are times when it makes sense to hunt specifically for bucks, particularly during the rut. There isn't much you can do to call a doe within shooting range during the hunting season. Doe-hunting tactics are almost purely opportunistic ambushes, whereas a buck can be summoned during the rut if you have the correct tools and have studied when and how to use them. Even meat hunters will hunt bucks now and then, so it pays to have an understanding of what makes them tick.

The most distinctive feature of a buck, at first glance, is obviously the antlers. Antlers are seasonal growths of bone that eventually drop off on an annual basis. They arise from *pedicles* — dense, circular clusters of cells on a buck's cranium that make bone cells at an astonishingly rapid rate. The pedicles first appear when the buck is just a few weeks old, and antlers begin to grow from the pedicles as soft, fuzzy lumps. The bone of the antlers needs a blood supply in order to grow, so it is covered with a soft, fuzzy material called *velvet*. The velvet carries blood to the growing antlers until they reach their full size, typically by midsummer. Antlers are the fastest-growing bones in the known world, sometimes growing by as much as an inch per day.

Antler size is largely determined by genetics, although quality of diet plays an important role as well. A high proportion of crude protein and calcium in the diet is important for bucks, both during and immediately after the growth of antlers. The nutrients that compose the antlers are provided mainly through daily diet, but a significant amount of calcium is obtained from the rest of the skeletal system in a process

Antlers versus Horns

ANTLERS ARE NOT THE SAME as horns. Horns are composed of keratin that is usually layered over a bony core. Keratin is a sort of general-purpose material that vertebrates use to grow anything needed on the skin. Scales, hair, fingernails, and hooves are all composed chiefly of keratin. The rhinoceros has a horn made solely of keratin, which sits in a socket in its face and is not directly connected to the skeleton at all. Most animals with horns, including all true antelopes, will keep them for life, and they will grow slowly but continuously. Antlers differ from horns in that they are pure bone with no keratin covering.

With the sole exception of the pronghorn, animals keep horns for life but shed antlers seasonally.

known as *resorption*. Most of the resorbed calcium and minerals is taken from the shoulder blades and the ribs. These bones are temporarily weakened until the buck consumes enough minerals to replace what was lost. Antler growth stops, and the velvet is shed as a result of increased testosterone levels in the deer's body.

Testosterone levels in bucks are regulated by the action of the pineal gland, an organ in the brain about the size of a pea that is influenced by the amount of daily sunlight perceived by the deer. As the photoperiod changes with the coming of autumn, the pineal gland effectively instructs the testes to increase testosterone output.

With this increase in testosterone, a number of changes happen that affect both the behavior and the physiology of a buck. First, the blood supply to the velvet is cut off. The velvet dies, and the buck rubs its antlers against a low-hanging branch or a sapling to scrape it off. The amount of blood remaining in the velvet and the pigment in the bark of the tree that he rubs against will help determine the colors of the finished antlers.

The buck's neck will begin to swell up and strengthen. He begins to spar in a friendly way with other bucks, testing the size of his weaponry relative to that of his neighbors. These fights will gradually become less friendly as the rut approaches, and the buck will become somewhat territorial. The buck will "spar" with trees and branches as well — anything to exercise and strengthen his neck. The longest antlers in the world won't do much good against a rival buck if the neck is not strong enough to support and maneuver those antlers in a fight.

When the rut is long over and the amount of daylight increases, the changing photoperiod prompts the pineal gland to signal the body to produce less testosterone. As testosterone levels decrease, the pedicles rapidly absorb the bone mass at the base of each antler. This is the same process of resorption that built the antlers in the first place. The result is that the unsupported antlers fall off. There may be a few drops of visible blood on the exposed pedicles, but skin grows over them very quickly.

The Pineal Gland

THE PINEAL GLAND is responsible for causing biological changes in animals based on changes in the seasons. The gland is located near the center of the brain in all vertebrates. Among mammals it is tied closely to signals from the retinas and is stimulated by the duration of daylight to produce chemicals such as melatonin, which in turn can cause other glands throughout the body to produce varying levels of hormones, including testosterone.

Its origins are quite strange. In our distant ancestry, the pineal gland was part of the anatomy of an entire third eye. This third eye is referred to as a *parietal eye*. A more complete version of the structure still appears in many lizards, fish, and amphibians. Usually, this parietal eye, if externally visible at all, looks like a gray speck on an animal's snout.

The most highly developed parietal eye among modern species is found in the tuatara, which looks like a lizard but is part of a group of reptiles that predates the dinosaurs by millions of years. At birth, a tuatara has a translucent patch of skin on top of its head through which a third eye is visible. This parietal eye has a lens and a cornea and is connected to the brain through the nervous system. Like the eyes of other animals, the tuatara's parietal eye detects light through a system of cells that is similar to but distinct from the rod-and-cone structure that other vertebrate eyes use. The parietal eye of a tuatara is covered over with scales by about 6 months of age, but its existence and its unique system of light detection suggest that even more distant ancestors had parietal eyes that were more complex and developed.

Why did those ancient vertebrates have three eyes? What was that extra eye for, and how did it come to evolve with a distinct system of light detection? We don't know. Yet it is a fact that there is an ancient lineage common to all vertebrates, including humans and whitetail deer, that includes a body plan having three eyes rather than the two per customer that we think of as standard. While that third eye is generally either invisible or nonexistent in modern vertebrates, the pineal gland that was once part of that system still plays an essential role in our lives. A deer without a pineal gland would have no means of coaxing its body to prepare for reproduction at the right time of year.

CHAPTER THREE

THE EVOLUTION OF DEER

Whitetail deer have been around in their present form for about 3 million years. This makes them the oldest extant species of deer in the world. There are two groups of animals that we refer to as deer: new-world deer and old-world deer. New-world deer include (among many others) whitetails, moose, and reindeer. Elk, red deer, and roe deer are all members of the old-world group. Bizarrely, these two groups are only distantly related and are the products of convergent evolution. Their last common ancestor was a forest-dwelling animal with sharp fangs and no antlers; it resembled the modern duiker antelope in physiology, and probably in its behavior as well.

Development of Antlers

O ver millions of years following the divergence of new- and old-world deer, both groups underwent nearly identical changes. In their feet, separate tibias and fibulas became fused into a single cannon bone, which is much more effective for accelerating rapidly to escape from predators. Both groups also developed antlers and lost their fangs.

This type of trade in weaponry is a common one in evolutionary biology. Fangs are for doing real damage to an opponent, potentially killing it. They are just the thing for a defender of scant material resources in a well-defined territory. Herbivores with fangs are typically loners, aside from mating and rearing their young. If another deer shows up, it must be chased away from the territory using whatever force is required.

Primitive deer had fighting fangs that gradually disappeared over generations, as antlers became more developed.

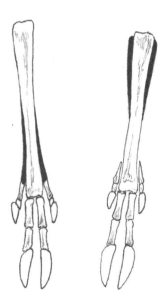

Old-world and new-world deer are distinguished by the bones of their lower limbs. Old-world deer (right) have a free-floating vestigial bone; among new-world deer (left), this bone is fused.

For a species to evolve into more sociable and herdlike behavior, it is essential that its members develop a way to establish a pecking order without a high risk of killing one another. This often means the evolution of hard protrusions from the head that can be used for wrestling. Antlers, horns, and perhaps specialized teeth, such as those found in the elephant and the babirusa, work well for nonfatal grappling. It is a general rule of thumb that as the antlers or horns get bigger through successive generations, the fangs will shrink.

It would be a mistake to consider antlers to be a more "advanced" adaptation than fangs, since at many points in the evolution of both new- and old-world deer it was necessary for them to become defenders of

The modern Chinese water deer has highly developed fangs and no antlers at all.

A muntjac has smaller fangs than a water deer, paired with rudimentary antlers.

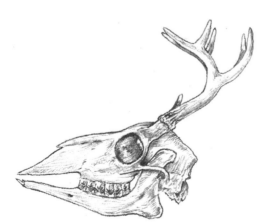

The whitetail has highly developed antlers and no remaining sign of fangs.

Mule deer (which are descended from whitetails) lack fangs and their antlers tend to be more branched than those of whitetails.

material resources once again, and antlers were traded back in for fangs. Even today there are many species of muntjac deer in Asia with long fangs and no antlers. For all we know, our native American whitetails could be fanged and bareheaded 10,000 years from now.

Thus it was that in response to very similar environmental pressures, the two groups of modern deer evolved in two ways, and more or less simultaneously. The two groups have moved around the world both naturally and through deliberate introduction by humans such that their geographic location does not necessarily say much about which group any given species belongs to. American elk came across the Bering land bridge from Asia only about 15,000 years ago.

Adapting to Environmental Changes

Whitetails have probably been around in their current form for so long because they are capable of colonizing and thriving in almost every environment in North America. During times of upheaval and changing climate, more specialized animals become extinct and leave habitat wide open for whitetails.

The one habitat where deer find it difficult to thrive is grasslands, such as the Great Plains and the Serengeti. This is unarguably the result of having antlers instead of horns. Antlers are shed annually, requiring the growth of a new set every year. Replacing such a high volume of bone year after year requires a diet that is, at least seasonally, very high in calcium compared to the diet of adult animals without antlers. Grasslands do not typically contain high concentrations of plants that are rich in calcium. Animals with horns, with the sole exception of the pronghorn, keep the same headgear year after year. Horns consist of a core of live bone covered in keratin (the same substance our fingernails are made of). Horns need to be grown only once, and usually this happens gradually over a period of years. Nutritionally, horns are the way to go for social animals living in grasslands.

POPULATION GROWTH

The population of whitetails has boomed during the last 40 years. Many factors contributed to this. One way of looking at the situation is that whitetail deer are doing what they have always done during times of environmental upheaval. It is only relatively recently that some of the whitetail's biggest competition for food and habitat in the eastern United States disappeared.

DECLINE IN COMPETING SPECIES. Bison were quite common along much of the East Coast during the early colonial era. We are accustomed to thinking of bison as animals that teemed in herds of tens or hundreds of thousands on the Great Plains, but there was a very common forest-dwelling subspecies here, once upon a time. In my home state of Virginia, the last wild bison was killed in 1801 by the youngest son of Daniel Boone. Bison made pretty easy targets for European colonists armed with muskets and rifles. They didn't run away as readily as deer and presented quite a lot of meat for people who were struggling to survive.

Wild elk, or wapiti, were also formerly far more common across the United States than they are today. Wild elk were extirpated from the eastern states by the late 1800s, although recently there have been successful efforts to reintroduce them to small areas.

INCREASE IN FOOD SUPPLY. Removing the bison and the elk from so much habitat left a lot of food available for whitetails, which were and remain much harder to hunt with firearms. Whitetails don't have exactly the same diet as those woodland bison probably did, but there is certainly enough crossover to provide a boon to the deer. When wolves were eliminated from most states by deliberate government policy and the eastern cougar was reduced to effective extinction around 1900, the stage was set for whitetails to take over. Most of the predators and the competition for food were gone.

HUMAN INFLUENCE ON THE ENVIRONMENT. Behaviorally, it seems to have taken a few decades for whitetails to adapt to living at the edges of ever-increasing human civilization. At the same time, we planted vast acres of crops that are higher in calcium, protein, and carbohydrates than are most native plants. Much of what had been grasslands became good deer country.

There does not appear to be an end in sight for the environmental and ecological upheaval that has been going on in North America for the last 15,000 years. Human beings continue to reshape the landscape and the very atmosphere. With each passing year, we add another shockingly high number of extinctions to the list. Generalist species, such as whitetails, will not be appearing on that list. The more upheaval we create in our environment, the more whitetail deer seem to thrive. Perhaps some of them will diversify into new species that are more specifically adapted to their environment.

Fewer Chestnuts = More Acorns

THE CHESTNUT BLIGHT during the early twentieth century may have eventually helped whitetails to increase their numbers. Before the American chestnuts began dying, in the early 1900s, they represented up to 25 percent of the trees in many eastern forests. As the fungus killed off those trees, they were replaced in part by higher numbers of the oak trees that had been in competition with them for space in the canopy. Deer did eat some of the chestnuts, but the necessity of removing the burrs makes chestnuts a more labor-intensive food compared to acorns. The death of the chestnut trees represented a temporary loss of food sources to deer; this may have had something to do with the decline in whitetail numbers that took place between 1900 and the 1950s.

Once the replacement oaks matured and began producing acorns, the result was probably more food available to deer per calories burned to glean it than had been the case prior to the chestnut blight.

PHYSICAL CHANGES

Global warming is likely to have some effect on whitetail society and behavior over the next century. Whitetails in warmer climates tend to have a longer rutting period, with the result that many fawns are born later in the spring. If the winters are warmer, it will be less crucial for fawns to enter winter with a maximum of weight put on. Those late fawns will survive, passing on their late-estrous genes to other generations. Whitetails may also become slightly smaller throughout most of their present range. There is a tendency among animals, known as Bergmann's rule, to have a larger body in colder climates than in warmer climates.

The long-term absence of large predators could allow deer to develop more "luxury" organs and coloration. Antlers could become bigger than what would really make sense for fast escapes through dense brush, and males could develop unique coloration or patterns that make them more distinct and visible to does. High deer densities could eventually result in does giving birth to single fawns rather than twins; or perhaps they might choose the healthier of the two to raise past a certain age while leaving the other to starve, as other animals (such as the brown pelican) do. If one larger, healthier fawn would be more likely to survive to pass on its genes than two scrawny fawns would, then it would make a terrible sort of sense to let one fawn die very early, even if the body insists on producing the pair of them.

Then again, perhaps having so many whitetails in competition for the same resources will lead to a disappearance of antlers entirely, in favor of growing fangs and defending a territory fiercely against other deer. The evolution of whitetail deer is a story that is continuing to unfold right in front of us.

Mule Deer and Blacktails

Whitetails are the most numerous and widely dispersed species of deer in North America, but there are some areas of the United States and Canada where whitetails are scarce or nonexistent. In those areas, you will often still find mule deer and blacktails.

EVOLUTION

Blacktail deer evolved from whitetails about 2 million years ago. Blacktails usually have somewhat larger bodies than whitetails, though the antlers are generally smaller. Today they are found along the Pacific coast from California to Alaska. As we move inland from the coast, blacktails tend to give way to the aptly named mule deer.

Mule deer, a widespread subspecies of blacktails, evolved only between 5,000 and 9,000 years ago as a result of interbreeding between whitetails and blacktails during a time when predators were scarce. They form part of a *cline* with the blacktails, which is to say that they interbreed at the edges of their ranges, creating a gradual shift in the appearance of the deer one would see while traveling inland. Mule deer are far more numerous and widespread than blacktails are. "Muleys" have large, showy antlers and a set of adaptive behaviors, shared somewhat with other blacktails, that affects their distribution and the methods used to hunt them.

At a glance, mule deer could easily be mistaken for whitetails. They have the same basic body type but are larger than either whitetails or blacktails. In geographic regions where they overlap with whitetails, they utilize the same food sources.

DIFFERENCES IN BEHAVIOR

The biggest differences between whitetails and blacktails are in their strategies for evading predators.

Whitetails tend to hide out in thick cover and suddenly spook at the approach of a predator. They rocket out from a standstill to top speed very quickly and tend to seek an escape route along a known, established trail while avoiding obstacles. A whitetail will usually run downhill or along level terrain and rely on pure speed to put so much distance between it and the predator that by the time the whitetail has tired and slowed, the scent is dispersed enough to make the deer impossible to find.

That behavior makes it difficult for a human hunter to have any real chance of shooting a whitetail once it has decided to run. You may have time for one very quick offhand shot if you've gotten quite close before spooking it. With no time to line up the shot perfectly, you have low odds of success. This is why people don't usually chase whitetails. The tactics described in this book focus on understanding the animals' needs and motivations to figure out where deer will be in the future so you can wait for them to show up. It doesn't work very well the other way around.

Mule deer and blacktails behave entirely differently. They are well adapted to steep hills. They are more likely to sneak silently away than they are to bolt when a potential predator approaches. And mule deer are much better at moving quietly than whitetails are. When they know they have been spotted, instead of running downhill, they will stot uphill.

Stotting describes the mule deer's stride for fast movement. The animal is capable of launching itself in high, forward bounds with a motion not unlike that of a pogo stick. This stride is much more efficient at quickly carrying the deer uphill than other strides are. It allows it to easily outpace any lone predator. Unlike whitetails, mule deer will deliberately seek out obstacles to jump over while running away. While they are certainly fast, their escape depends largely on taking the pursuer on a chase that's too difficult to follow. Agility, rather than speed, is the key to their survival.

Mule deer will frequently stop while running away in order to turn around and briefly see what the predator is doing. This trait makes it worth shouldering your rifle immediately if you should chance to spook a mule deer. You may get lucky and have the opportunity for a shot. Whitetails rarely exhibit the same behavior.

Blacktails and mule deer are more likely to challenge and attack a predator directly. Mule deer bucks, in particular, will often confront lone coyotes and drive them away. If the confrontation is not going well, a mule deer has the option of escaping uphill at a speed faster than it can usually be pursued.

This set of responses to predation generally limits mule deer to hilly terrain, with the exception of areas where natural predators have been largely eliminated by humans. In flat or gently sloped country, the stotting stride is not an effective means of escape.

Because of the steep terrain, hunting mule deer is often a physical challenge. Hunters will be most successful if they climb to near the top of a hill or mountain and "glass" for their prey by sitting on a good vantage point and looking around with a decent pair of binoculars. With relatively little cover and few trees in the desert and sagebrush country of much of their range, mule deer can be seen from quite a distance. Hunters will often need to take longer shots than what is required when hunting whitetails and should be prepared with a rifle and scope that are equal to the task, as well as a lot of target practice.

LIFE CYCLES

The annual life cycles of mule deer and blacktails are very similar to that of the whitetail. They share the habits of closely coordinating birth of fawns and of alternately gathering together and dispersing at different times of the year. The chief difference is that mule deer does with fawns tend not to seek out the company of their matriarchal group until later in the year, when the fawns are more mature.

Blood tracking, field dressing, and butchering are all treated identically among these three groups of deer.

BLACKTAIL DEER

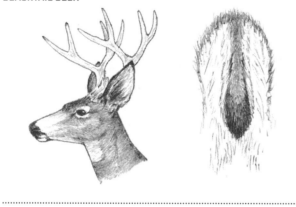

Blacktails tend to have smaller antlers and bodies than mule deer do, and the black coloration on the back of the tail extends higher.

MULE DEER

CHAPTER FOUR

CHOOSE YOUR WEAPON

There's no getting around the fact that you'll need some kind of weapon to hunt deer. Our distant ancestors may have started out running down antelope on wide-open grasslands in the same manner that some bushmen still do in the Kalahari Desert. A sharp stick or a rock works just fine on a winded animal as it lies exhausted on the ground, but as early humans moved into other environments, they found that different tactics and weapons were called for. You will have to make a similar judgment about what weapon to use where you will be hunting. The principal factors to consider are the laws and regulations, the habitat, and the value of your own time.

Learn Your Local Regulations

B efore purchasing your first weapon, you should find out what the legal requirements are for its purchase and possession. Any weapon capable of killing a deer is going to be subject to special regulations somewhere in the United States. For example, in the state of North Carolina, a handgun permit is required to purchase a crossbow (this is unusual). In my home state of Virginia, however, not only can crossbows be sold over the counter to any adult, but there is no such thing as a handgun permit (instead, Virginia conducts especially thorough background checks at the time of purchase). Obviously, laws regulating weapons vary tremendously from one place to another, so you'll need to contact your state wildlife agency to find out what you will or won't be able to purchase legally, let alone be permitted to hunt with.

You'll also need to make sure that the laws in the place where you intend to hunt will allow you to hunt with the weapon you're purchasing. For example, you could walk into a sporting goods store in Illinois and purchase a fine bolt-action deer rifle. But the State of Illinois requires that deer be hunted only with archery equipment or shotguns.

Nearly everything you need to know about state and local hunting regulations can be learned by reading the information on the website of your state's game or wildlife department. You'll learn even more by taking a hunter education class.

Pay close attention to a few key issues when researching your state and local regulations. Some places require a permit to purchase or possess any firearm, and you will have to obtain that permit first. Requiring a permit to buy a rifle or shotgun is not the norm in the United States, but some states and municipalities have laws to that effect. Look closely at different designations offered on hunting licenses for different fees. Usually, there will be a basic license that allows small game to be taken; then deer and other prey can be added to the license for an additional fee. Finally, pay attention to the exact dates that hunting seasons begin and end in your area. This can change from year to year, and there are many different seasons. Every species that can be hunted will have specific dates during which particular weapons can or cannot be used.

HUNTING SEASONS	CALENDAR	SEASONS IN THE LIFE CYCLES OF DEER
In most states, hunting isn't allowed from March through August.	JAN FEB **MAR** APR MAY JUN JUL AUG SEP OCT NOV DEC	Spring marks the beginning of antler growth.
	JAN FEB MAR APR **MAY JUN** JUL AUG SEP OCT NOV DEC	Fawning is usually from mid-May to early June.
	JAN FEB MAR APR MAY JUN **JUL** AUG SEP OCT NOV DEC	Fawns are usually weaned by 8 to 10 weeks.
	JAN FEB MAR APR MAY JUN JUL **AUG SEP** OCT NOV DEC	In late summer into fall, antler growth stops and velvet is shed.
Archery seasons generally begin in September.	JAN FEB MAR APR MAY JUN JUL AUG **SEP** OCT NOV DEC	September marks the beginning of the pre-rut.
October and early November mark muzzleloader hunting in most states.	JAN FEB MAR APR MAY JUN JUL AUG SEP **OCT NOV** DEC	Peak of the rut.
General firearm season is during November and December in most of the country. Occasionally a state will have a late archery or muzzleloading season in late fall.	JAN FEB MAR APR MAY JUN JUL AUG SEP OCT **NOV DEC**	Rump rut may occur.
	JAN FEB MAR APR MAY JUN JUL AUG SEP OCT NOV **DEC**	Most bucks begin to shed their antlers in December.

HUNTER EDUCATION

Hunter education classes are now required for almost everyone who purchases a hunting license in most of the American states and Canadian provinces. There are exemptions in some states for people who were born prior to a certain date or in some cases if you are hunting on your own land. You should take the class, regardless of whether you're required to. In most states, the class is regularly offered free of charge. While it's not designed to teach you how to be successful as a hunter, it will be very good at teaching you what the local laws are and how to avoid hurting yourself or others while hunting. It also serves as a great opportunity to get answers to your hunting-related questions from knowledgeable people.

A Comparison of Firearms

Since you're hunting for food and not for sport, using a firearm (rather than a bow; see page 84) is the most practical and efficient option. There are four broad categories of firearms that are used to hunt deer: shotguns, muzzleloaders, pistols, and rifles.

Hunters who pursue deer with shotguns almost always do so because some state or local law prohibits them from using a rifle. The rifle is the better tool for the job, without question. Some of those who use muzzleloaders enjoy the history of the technology and the challenge involved with it, although most are just trying to hunt for a few extra weeks during a special muzzleloader-only season. Pistols are favored by a relative few, including people with disabilities that prevent them from using both arms; hunters who will be traveling a very long way through rough country and want to reduce weight and encumbrance; and advanced hunters who are looking for a new challenge. A modern rifle is the usual and ideal tool with which to hunt deer in terms of pure practicality.

All modern firearms work like a little rocket ship that goes sideways. With the exception of most muzzleloaders, the trigger releases a spring-driven firing pin that smacks into a chemical called a *primer*. The primer makes a little "bang" when it is struck, and the bang ignites the gunpowder. As it burns, the gunpowder quickly turns from a solid into a rapidly expanding gas, which then forces the projectile (either a single bullet or a lot of smaller spheres of shot) down the barrel.

Before we look at each of these weapons in depth, definitions are in order.

RIFLES

What we typically refer to as a rifle these days is a weapon that usually has a barrel of no less than 16 inches, with a stock that fits against the shoulder to stabilize the weapon for better aim, and which can be loaded with prepared ammunition through an opening in the middle of the weapon. A rifle is so named for the "rifling" on the inside of the barrel. Rifling is a set of spiraling grooves cut into the inside of the barrel that cause the bullet to spin as it travels towards its target, making it more accurate (think about the stability gained by a gyroscope when it spins). This was a big improvement over the "smoothbore" muskets that were once common. Most handguns also now have rifled barrels, as do modern muzzleloaders and certain types of shotguns. There are two features of rifling to keep track of: the *grooves* and the *lands*. The grooves are the valleys of the rifling, and the lands are the peaks.

Scoped revolvers, shotguns, bolt-action rifles, and muzzleloaders can all be practical weapons for hunting deer.

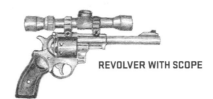

REVOLVER WITH SCOPE

SHOTGUN WITH RIFLED BARREL AND SCOPE MOUNT

BOLT-ACTION RIFLE

PLAINS-STYLE PERCUSSION MUZZLELOADER RIFLE

SHOTGUNS

A shotgun is a long-barreled weapon with
a stock like a rifle has. Superficially, it looks
very much like a rifle but is used much differently. A shotgun is usually intended as a
tool for hitting moving targets. To this end, a
shotgun is normally loaded with a cylindrical
plastic cartridge containing many small lead
or steel spheres that are referred to as *shot*
or *pellets*. Bigger prey requires larger shot,
which is referred to as *buckshot*.

SABOT ROUND WITH SLEEVE

RIFLED SLUG

hull

wad

powder

brass

primer

BUCKSHOT

*Shotshells can be loaded with
various types of projectiles for
different applications.*

Shotguns normally have smoothbored
barrels with no rifling. (A rifled barrel would
cause the shot to come flying out of the barrel
in a sort of long, stringy pattern rather than in
the uniform cloud of shot that is more likely
to hit a target.) A shotgun is not usually aimed
in the carefully targeted manner that a rifle is.
The art of the shotgunner is to make a cloud
of moving shot pellets intersect with a moving
object in midair. A shotgun is pointed, swung, and fired in an instinctual
manner. Thinking about it too much will result in a miss.

Imagine holding a garden hose and trying to spray a kid running
past you about 10 yards away. You can't aim the hose right at him, because
the water isn't moving that fast. What you would find yourself doing is
spraying *ahead* of where you see the runner, while moving the hose along
his trajectory slightly faster than he's moving. This is the essence of the
shotgunning technique.

The diameter of that moving cloud of shot pellets is very important
to the shotgunner. Hunters become concerned with how quickly that cloud
of pellets expands outward as it moves. For example, if you were shooting
at a dove that's 35 yards away and your shotgun tends to make a cloud of
30 pellets open up to 3 feet in diameter, the gaps in that cloud of pellets are
big enough that the dove could go right through it without being hit. Yet if
your pattern of shot is too tight, you will find that it is especially difficult to
hit fast-moving targets that are only 15 yards away.

The size and distribution of these patterns of shot can be controlled by something called a *choke*. The choke of a shotgun is a point near the end of the barrel where its inside diameter becomes slightly tighter right before the shot leaves. Some shotguns have a fixed choke built into the barrel, whereas others have threads cut into the metal of the barrel so interchangeable choke tubes can be used, depending on the prey or the expected distances to be encountered.

The use of shotguns to hunt deer has resulted in some quite specialized shotguns that have come to resemble rifles in both use and hardware. Buckshot is not usually the ideal kind of shot to hunt deer with, because its effective range is limited to perhaps 30 yards at most. At close range, buckshot can be devastating, but misjudging the distance can result in a horribly wounded deer that runs away to die slowly of its injuries. Buckshot may be used when hunting deer in very thick brush, where any shot opportunity will be at close range with no time to really aim and where the deer will probably start moving before you even see it.

SLUG GUNS. If you must use a shotgun for hunting deer, it's best to use a slug gun. *Slugs* are essentially very big lead bullets loaded into a shotshell. Although accuracy is usually poor compared to that of rifle bullets and the recoil is fierce, the effective range is superior to buckshot in both accuracy and penetration. Among solid slugs there are two basic varieties: rifled slugs and sabot slugs.

RIFLED SLUGS are so named because they have rifling molded into them, which is supposed to work like the rifling on the inside of a rifle barrel. They're meant to be used with smoothbore shotguns. In truth, the rifling on these slugs does absolutely nothing to stabilize the path of the slug. This design may have started out as a legitimate attempt at making a more accurate slug, but today it is pure marketing gimmickry. Rifled slugs actually do have a more stable flight path than, say, an old-fashioned round ball fired out of a smoothbore musket barrel, but this is the result of a slug's being molded into an odd shape with a lot of weight in front and a wide, scooped-out back end that has a ballistic effect similar to that of a badminton shuttlecock in flight.

SABOT SLUGS are essentially oversize rifle bullets that are a little smaller than the diameter of the shotgun's barrel. Each slug is wrapped in a plastic sleeve, or *sabot,* which has a diameter that is slightly greater than the inside diameter of the shotgun barrel. Sabot slugs are intended for use in shotguns with barrels that have been rifled like the barrel of a rifle. The plastic sabot engages tightly with the rifling inside the barrel to impart a controlled spin on the slug, which stabilizes it in flight. This sabot separates from the slug after it leaves the barrel.

A sabot slug is capable of much better accuracy than a rifled slug. You may be able to shoot groups of five shots as tight as 3 or 4 inches at 100 yards off a very steady rest. The catch is that they work that well only when fired from a rifled shotgun barrel. If you use sabot slugs in a regular shotgun, there's no rifling for the sabot to engage with, and accuracy will be no better than rifled slugs and possibly worse — for twice the price.

Shotguns can be scoped or fitted with open sights, just like a rifle. In fact, there are even bolt-action shotguns. Because there's a market of people living in shotgun-only states, many firearms manufacturers have produced slug guns that mimic rifles as closely as possible, while still technically being considered shotguns. Indeed, one may wonder exactly what the difference is between a conventional deer rifle and a slug gun with a rifled barrel, scope, and magazine full of sabot slugs.

The differences are recoil, effective range, and accuracy. One hundred yards is the maximum limit for a reliably accurate shot from all but the most advanced and well-tuned slug guns. The slug does keep going beyond that distance, so if you get just the right equipment and find just the right ammunition, you might be able to increase your accuracy as far out as 150 yards: that is, if the effect of the recoil on your shooting posture doesn't limit you to a fraction of that. Twelve-gauge slugs kick hard — I've had to use them on a few occasions, and I cannot imagine how a handicapped, a small-stature, or an elderly person could be expected to hunt with such a thing.

The addition of a better recoil pad may help somewhat. A recoil pad either slips on or is permanently attached to the butt of the gun to absorb some of the recoil. If the recoil of a 12-gauge slug is still too much for you, move down to a 20-gauge shotgun.

GAUGE AND CALIBER are two terms that may be confusing to a beginning hunter. Perhaps counterintuitively, the gauge number of a shotgun is higher for smaller-diameter barrels; the gauges originally referred to the number of lead balls for a given barrel size (as measured by its diameter) that could be cast from a single pound of lead. For a 20-gauge shotgun, for example, a pound of lead makes 20 balls. This was the common British nomenclature for most firearm calibers, but the usage has survived only among shotguns. The sole exception to this system for shotguns is the diminutive .410 bore, a relatively recent invention named for its actual diameter of 0.41 inch. Slugs for a .410 do exist but are inadequate for hunting deer.

Caliber refers to a measurement of the diameter of the barrel or bullet. A .30-caliber bullet is 0.3 inch in diameter. Keep in mind, however, that caliber is only one of many specifications of a firearm cartridge. Both the .30-06 and the .308 cartridges fire bullets of the same diameter, but those types of ammunition are still not interchangeable.

If you must use a shotgun, try to get one with a slug barrel, and be sure to put a scope on it. If you already have a shotgun, find out if there is a replacement slug barrel available for your particular model.

There are two types of slug barrels: The first is a *smoothbore,* like a regular shotgun barrel, distinguished by its open-cylinder choke (this means that the muzzle end of the barrel does not contract slightly to control the spread of a cloud of pellets, the way most shotgun barrels do) and often by riflelike open sights or a scope mount. The smoothbore barrel will work adequately, but poor accuracy will limit your range to 75 yards. The second type — rifled slug barrel — will be more accurate and is the better way to go.

Unlike most rifle barrels, many shotgun barrels can be swapped out and replaced at home without the tools or skills of a gunsmith. Many old pump-action Mossberg and Remington shotguns are especially easy to modify in this manner. With a new barrel, a scope, and a good recoil pad, such a shotgun can be turned into a reasonably effective gun for deer. It still won't be as good as a rifle, but it will work.

Shotguns are usually used to hunt deer only because some law or regulation requires it. Slug guns are really just engineering solutions to a regulatory problem. Few hunters would choose to hunt deer with a slug gun if rifles are permitted.

MUZZLELOADERS

The final category of long gun to be considered in hunting deer is the *muzzleloader*. A muzzleloader is an archaic type of firearm that does not use cartridges. Instead, the proper amount of gunpowder is poured down the barrel from the muzzle end and a bullet or ball is rammed on top of it, using a *ramrod*.

Many people hunt during muzzleloader season with faithful reproductions of muzzleloader rifles used during the 1700s and 1800s. Others use more modern devices fitted with scopes and synthetic stocks that meet the minimal legal definition of a muzzleloader. Some states do not allow these modern updates to the muzzleloader design for hunting

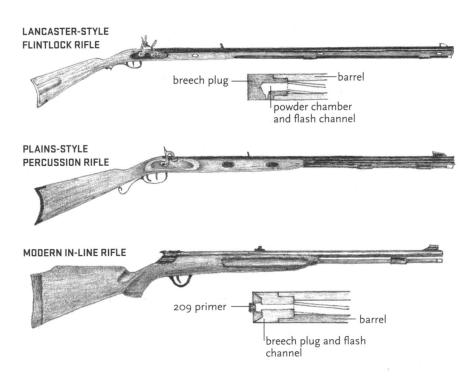

LANCASTER-STYLE
FLINTLOCK RIFLE

breech plug — barrel

powder chamber
and flash channel

PLAINS-STYLE
PERCUSSION RIFLE

MODERN IN-LINE RIFLE

209 primer — barrel

breech plug and flash
channel

There are different types of muzzleloaders that use varying means of igniting the gunpowder.

purposes. Suffice it to say that the world of muzzleloading rifles in the United States is a very large and convoluted one.

If you live in an area that allows both modern muzzleloaders and shotguns but not modern rifles, you might be better off using a modern muzzleloader. Although they are fussy to clean (and must be cleaned almost religiously, because of the destructive effects of the black powder residue on metal) and very slow to reload, the typical entry-level modern muzzleloader is unarguably more accurate than similarly priced slug guns. If you can trust yourself to clean the inside of the barrel without fail every single time you shoot it, a muzzleloader could be a smart option.

The practice of hunting deer with a muzzleloader is not necessarily very different from hunting with a modern rifle. The biggest difference is that because of the amount of time it takes to reload a muzzleloader, chances are you won't be able to take a follow-up shot. If the first shot didn't do the trick, it's extremely unlikely that the deer will still be hanging around long enough for you to get off another shot.

IN-LINE MUZZLELOADERS. Modern muzzleloaders usually have what is called an *in-line ignition system*. In-line muzzleloaders have everything important enclosed so the powder will stay dry even when you're hunting in bad weather. This is a design that could have been produced with the technology of the 1700s if it had occurred to anyone. In terms of pure practicality, the in-line system is superior to the older designs. The older systems, such as flintlocks, will not go *bang* when you need them to if the powder gets wet. Many people are traditionalists for aesthetic reasons, though, and prefer an old-fashioned system that faithfully reproduces the firearms of 200 years ago. Some states prohibit the use of in-line muzzle-loaders because of the demands of the traditionalists that everyone else hunt like they do during the muzzleloader season.

HANDGUNS

Relatively few people hunt deer with a handgun. As with bow hunting, people tend to take this up as a way of making hunting more challenging. Others (such as law enforcement officers) may have had extensive training with handguns and are simply more comfortable with that type of shooting. Some people may have a physical disability affecting one arm or hand that makes using a handgun more practical. A wounded veteran with only one arm would have a hard time shooting a long gun such as a rifle or shotgun but may be able to handle a .357 Magnum handgun just fine.

When handguns are used to hunt deer, they tend to be either revolvers or very specialized single-shot pistols. Among common pistol cartridges for deer are the .357 Magnum and the .44 Magnum. Long barrels are preferred, and many hunting pistols are equipped with a scope. Semiautomatic handguns that are purchased for self-defense rarely make very practical hunting weapons for deer. The sights tend to be crude and ammunition that performs well on deer is unlikely to be available for the cartridges such weapons are chambered for.

The practical range of most hunting pistols is about 50 yards (although there are some extremely talented people who have taken deer with revolvers at much greater ranges). Like a shotgun loaded with buckshot, a pistol can be a very practical tool for hunting in very thick brush where the shots will always be close. Not having a long barrel that snags on every branch can also be practical. However, a pistol is not a very flexible tool for hunting under a variety of circumstances. Across a 200-yard field, a .357 Magnum would be unlikely to hit a deer. Even if it did, there may not be enough velocity remaining to carry the bullet into a vital organ.

Rifles

For a new hunter in an area where you can hunt with any type of weapon that you choose, the most practical option is a rifle. Rifles represent a very large category of weapon. Even among those marketed as *deer rifles*, there's a lot to sort through as you consider which one might be the best for you.

ACTION TYPES

There are several different basic types of hunting rifle suitable for deer. The first thing that generally distinguishes them is the action type. The *action* of a rifle is sort of its mechanical heart — it's the main body of the rifle, onto which a barrel, stock, and sometimes a magazine are attached. A rifle's action usually (with the exception of a single-shot rifle) has a mechanical means of grabbing a cartridge from the magazine, loading it into the chamber of the barrel, locking it firmly into place, then driving a firing pin into the primer of the cartridge when the trigger is pulled. Afterward, it will extract the empty brass casing from the chamber before loading the next cartridge.

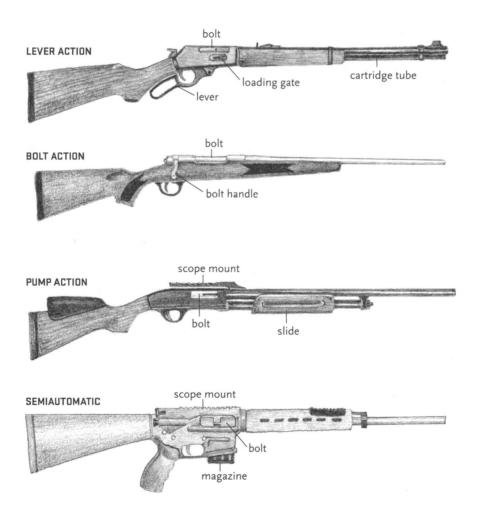

Modern rifles have various action types. All can be used to hunt deer, though each has its pros and cons.

BOLT ACTION. The most common action for hunting rifles is the *bolt action*. Bolt-action rifles have a handle that the shooter grasps with the dominant hand in order to operate the mechanism. This is considered an especially accurate and dependable type of action. The downside is that it is slower to operate than other action types.

LEVER ACTION. You may have seen *lever-action* rifles in old cowboy movies; they involve the use of a lever on the underside of the rifle to provide energy for the extraction and loading of cartridges. Many people find that they can operate a lever action faster than they can a bolt action. The primary attraction of a lever gun, however, may simply be an aesthetic one, depending on how much time you spent watching cowboy movies as a kid. They do have the advantage of being easier to operate without taking your eye too far away from the scope or sights.

Lever actions have two noteworthy disadvantages. It's more difficult to shoot a lever-action rifle from the prone position (lying on your stomach with elbows on the ground), because the lever is on the bottom of the rifle. (I've never taken a shot at a deer from the prone position because of the presence of vegetation that would block my shot, but some people find it necessary.)

The other problem is that your choice of bullets is very limited with many lever actions, because of their tubular magazine. A tubular magazine stores the cartridges in a straight line, end to end. Recoil could cause the tip of a bullet to indent the primer of the cartridge in front of it, essentially turning the rifle into a pipe bomb. To prevent this, most cartridges for lever guns are loaded with blunt-tipped bullets that are less aerodynamic and thus have more limited range than other bullets. One manufacturer (Hornady) now offers a patented bullet with a flexible plastic tip that cannot indent a primer but still provides the aerodynamic qualities of a pointed bullet. Needless to say, if you choose to use a lever-action rifle, your choices of ammunition will be limited by this issue. Older lever actions often lack the safety features found on later versions of the same models.

SEMIAUTOMATIC. A *semiautomatic action* is a clever device that uses energy from the firing of the first cartridge to automatically eject the spent casing and chamber the next cartridge without your having to work the bolt manually. This is different from a fully automatic action in the sense that one still has to pull the trigger again for the next cartridge to fire. Fully automatic weapons will keep firing as long as the trigger is depressed.

A semiauto has pros and cons as a hunting rifle. The main advantage of this action type is that you don't need to take your eye from the scope or divert your attention before taking the next shot. With bolt actions and to some extent lever actions, you must reacquire the target in the sights or scope for each shot. You can stay right on target with a semi-auto (depending on how much the recoil affects you). When hunting in or near heavy brush, this can be important. The difference between 1 second and 3 seconds between the first and second shots can be the difference between getting in a follow-up shot that puts a wounded animal down in its tracks and dealing with a deer that makes it into thick cover where you will have to track it for hours.

The negatives are more numerous. Semiautos tend to have more moving parts and are more of a hassle to disassemble and clean than bolt actions. They are also inherently less accurate. Most new bolt-action hunting rifles and many lever actions are capable of putting five shots within a 1-inch circle at 100 yards. Typical accuracy with semiautos is more like five shots in a 2- or 3-inch circle at the same distance. At longer ranges, this drift can be the difference between a good hit and a bad one. Semiautos are also somewhat more prone to jams and mechanical problems, although this varies by model.

If you have no strong feelings or preferences one way or another, I recommend that you get yourself a bolt-action rifle. There are more models of hunting rifles with more options and sizes available in bolt actions than in any other action type.

Among good, reasonably priced bolt-action rifles are the Remington Model 700, Weatherby's Vanguard, the Marlin XL-7 and XS-7, and the Savage 110. All are available in youth-size stocks that will fit hunters under 5'6" tall better than would a full-size stock.

FOUR

FITTING YOUR RIFLE

Whatever rifle you choose, make sure it fits you. You cannot do your best shooting if the distance between the butt of the stock and the trigger is too great (this distance is referred to as the *length of pull*). If you find yourself reaching so far that your dominant arm is hardly bent at all, the length of pull on that stock is too long. Also consider that most deer hunting is done in weather cold enough to wear a thick jacket. When you size up a stock, you should consider the effect that this extra padding will have on your length of pull.

RIFLES FOR WOMEN

It's unfortunate that most manufacturers of hunting equipment and clothing have not noticed the fact that women are the fastest-growing demographic group among hunters. Fifty years ago there were very few female hunters, but this is no longer the case. In families that hunt, daughters are now just as likely to go hunting as sons are. Until rifle makers wake up to this, adult women are forced to choose between youth rifles and full-size rifles that were designed for men between 5'8" and 6' tall.

A youth rifle is usually one with a short action, designed to use shorter cartridges, such as the .308 Winchester, the .243, or the 7 mm-08. A short, no-frills action is usually paired with a composite (plastic) stock that is an inch or two shorter than the standard stock. These rifles will work well enough for women of normal height. The problem is that the assumption when making these rifles is that they are for more or less temporary use until the hunter physically grows out of them and then goes shopping for a new rifle, so they usually lack options for many of the features that adult rifles have, such as a nice walnut stock, a wide variety of available cartridges, and an advanced corrosion-resistant finish on the barrel and action.

Cartridges Explained

It is easy to think of the rifle as the most important piece of equipment for hunting deer, but the cartridge fired by that rifle is the first thing to think about. The choice of a cartridge should come first, followed by the rifle. Keep in mind that the effect on the deer is governed entirely by the cartridge; the rifle is merely a delivery system, for the most part. How much weight of lead hits the animal in a given spot with how much force? How far can it penetrate, and can it reach and destroy a vital organ from a given angle?

These factors are almost entirely a question of the cartridge. The rifle is largely an ergonomic device that helps you place that bullet very carefully where it needs to be to do what it is capable of. The trade-off for higher performance is often recoil and cost. Start with the cartridge, then figure out what rifle you would like to use to deliver it.

HOW CARTRIDGES WORK

A rifle cartridge is composed of four basic elements: *case, powder, bullet,* and *primer.* The shiny, hollow brass casing (or *shell*) has a limited volume, within which is contained smokeless gunpowder. The case cannot be completely filled with powder, because there needs to be some room left in the neck, where the bullet is seated in the opening. At the other end there is a primer fastened snugly into the base. A primer is a tiny device containing a chemical that produces a bit of spark and heat when it is struck directly with sufficient force.

When the firing pin of the rifle hits the primer, the primer ignites, which lights the gunpowder. The gunpowder starts to burn within the confined space of the casing and hot gases are generated. As those gases rapidly expand, they force the bullet forward, out of the mouth of the case and down the barrel of the rifle. Gunpowder, blasted

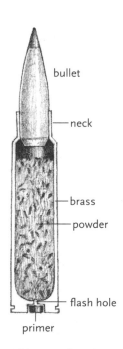

bullet

neck

brass

powder

flash hole

primer

A cartridge, seen here in cross section, is like a rocket ship that travels sideways.

forward by the initial explosion, continues to burn behind the bullet during these milliseconds, and the bullet continues to accelerate as it travels through the barrel.

You won't need to give much thought to primers and powder unless you decide to start loading your own ammunition (which many people do). But anyone who intends to hunt deer should have at least a basic understanding of the relative characteristics of different cases and bullets. This bears directly on how much force a bullet will strike its target with and what it will do to that target after it hits — an essential subject for anyone who wants to take down a deer with as little suffering as possible.

WHY CARTRIDGE CHOICE MATTERS

A rifle and its cartridge are a means of delivering pounds of energy at a prescribed speed into a deer's vital organ in order to disrupt that organ's normal function. Because deer do not walk around with their heart or spinal column on the outside of their body, your bullet will have to be carried by enough energy to pass through hide, fat, muscle, and bone

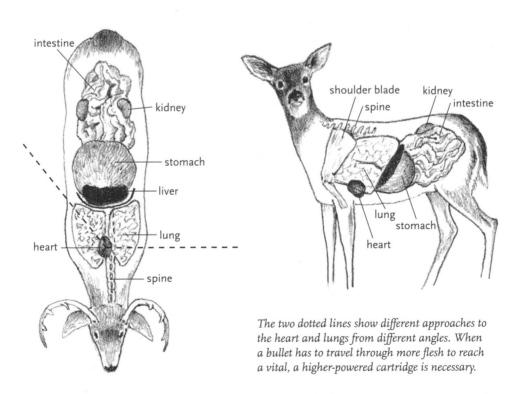

intestine

kidney

stomach

liver

lung

heart

spine

shoulder blade

spine

kidney

intestine

lung

stomach

heart

The two dotted lines show different approaches to the heart and lungs from different angles. When a bullet has to travel through more flesh to reach a vital, a higher-powered cartridge is necessary.

on its way to the heart. The total depth of tissue to penetrate en route to a vital organ changes significantly depending on what angle the deer is standing at relative to you. This is where the practical differences among the many cartridges and rifles on the rack at the gun store begin to assert themselves.

A dependable combination of cartridge and rifle will be capable of killing a deer from a variety of angles and — importantly— distances. After all, bullets lose energy while traveling through the air. Both gravity and friction against the air guarantee that a bullet will slow down before it hits its target. Most expert hunters agree that the minimum impact needed to be delivered to a deer-size animal for a reliable kill is about 1,000 foot-pounds of energy.

Generally speaking, a cartridge case that has a larger volume filled with powder is capable of propelling a bullet farther and faster than a smaller cartridge case loaded with the same type of powder and bullet. Not only will the larger case full of powder make the bullet go faster, but the increase in speed means that the ballistic arc of the bullet will be flatter and thus simpler to aim at varying ranges as well.

BALLISTIC ARC. What's a ballistic arc? Think about the difference between pitching a baseball as hard as you can and lobbing it. Pitching it hard makes the ball travel in a straighter line on its way. Lobbing the ball results in a trajectory shaped more like a rainbow.

CARTRIDGE	VELOCITY (FEET PER SECOND)			ENERGY (FOOT-POUNDS)			HOLDOVER AMOUNT (INCHES)
	At muzzle	At 100 yards	At 200 yards	At muzzle	At 100 yards	At 200 yards	At 200 yards
20-gauge sabot	1900	1615	—	2084	1506	—	—
.243 caliber pointed soft-point	3350	2955	2593	1993	1551	1194	1.6
30-06 caliber pointed soft-point	2910	2617	2342	2820	2281	1827	2.1
30-30 caliber pointed soft-point	2200	1895	1019	1827	1355	989	8.3

Different projectiles can have very different trajectories, with different points of impact at varying distances.

It is much easier to aim a bullet with a flatter ballistic trajectory: you can point the rifle right at the thing you are trying to shoot, rather than having to point the rifle somewhat above it, with the amount of holdover varying based on the exact distance to the target. (*Holdover* means that you are holding the crosshairs of the scope above the target, knowing that the bullet will drop that amount over the distance between you and the target. When no holdover is necessary, this is known as *point-blank* range.) The bigger the cartridge case the better, then, right? Not necessarily.

RECOIL

Bigger cases filled with more powder, especially those that also have larger bullets, will generate more recoil than smaller ones. Sir Isaac Newton pointed out that for every action there is an equal and opposite reaction. When a unit of mass (the bullet) is thrown from the barrel of your rifle, the rifle moves back against your shoulder with equal force. The mass of the rifle resists some of this motion, meaning that a heavier rifle will generate less recoil than a lighter one with the same cartridge.

Recoil can *really* be a problem. Nobody can do his best shooting with heavy recoil, but recoil seems to bother some people more than others. Overall stature probably has something to do with it; a person weighing 250 pounds can comfortably absorb more recoil than someone weighing 100 pounds. Practice and habit also figure into how much recoil affects you. The first time I shot a deer rifle, I ended up with a bruise on my shoulder for a week afterward. After shooting several thousand practice rounds, I am no longer bothered by the recoil of any standard deer cartridge. Shooting full-power 12-gauge shotgun slugs, however, still makes me want to cry and run home to ice my shoulder.

The pain recoil inflicts is only one part of the problem. Not only does recoil hurt at the time, but also repeated exposure to heavy recoil will make you develop a flinch in the instant before the rifle goes off. This flinching moves the whole rifle in your hands and throws off your point of aim.

There are hunting situations where recoil must be endured and dealt with. For example, if you're planning to face down a charging Cape buffalo in Africa, you certainly want to be prepared with a beast of a big-game rifle that will drop the buffalo (and knock your socks off) before he turns you into compost. However, there is room for compromise. There is a large spectrum of cartridges in between "elephants" and "mice" that includes plenty of options that are acceptable for deer, depending on issues such as the distance you are expecting between yourself and the deer.

LARGE VERSUS SMALL CARTRIDGES

If you'll be hunting in a heavily wooded area where visibility is rarely more than 50 yards, you have little need for the high velocity of larger cartridges. A bullet can lose only so much energy over the course of 50 yards. Cartridges such as the .30-30, 7.62 × 39, and 6.5 mm Swedish all do very well on deer over a shorter range, while having low power and comparatively little recoil.

There are some magnum cartridges that do very well over a long range but literally fall apart on a close shot, most notably the 7 mm Remington Magnum. This is a cartridge that has far greater sales in wooded areas of the country than it has any right to. The "7 Mag," as it's called, pushes a relatively light bullet very fast to strike a target several hundred yards out with close to 2,000 foot-pounds of energy at the moment of impact. But if a deer shows up a mere 25 yards away, the bullet will be moving so fast (around 3,500 feet per second) that on impact it can fragment against the side of the deer. This will cause only a superficial wound, and the deer will run away.

The 7 Mag might be a good choice for people hunting in wide-open spaces with potential shots out to 300 or 400 yards. Even then, you'll have to become a truly expert marksman to have any chance to make shots out that far under field conditions.

I have witnessed the results of a similar effect following the use of the .243 Winchester on a deer at about 80 yards away. The hunter took what should have been a perfect heart shot, but the small bullet was still going so fast at that short range that it blew up into shrapnel against the deer's shoulder. With so little mass in the first place, there was no single piece of lead large enough to penetrate the body cavity of the deer. Only a lucky head shot happened to bring down the running deer a few seconds later.

I autopsied the wound in the course of butchering the deer, and what I saw was quite convincing. There's such a thing as too much velocity when hunting deer. If that same bullet had hit the same spot at 150 or 200 yards, the deer may have gone down. But who wants to pass up a shot because the deer is too close? For this reason, I'm not a big fan of the .243 for deer. If you must use it, look for ammunition loaded with particularly heavy bullets.

COST AND AVAILABILITY

Within the parameters of a cartridge that delivers sufficient energy to a deer without a needless amount of recoil, there are probably hundreds of cartridges on the books that meet the need. We will narrow them down by considering a few other practical parameters: cost and availability of ammunition, as well as the availability of rifles that are chambered for the cartridge.

This last point is a key reason it's important to choose a cartridge before you select a rifle. You wouldn't want to find yourself in a position where you've invested hundreds of dollars in a rifle, only to discover that 2 years later nobody is selling the ammo for it. Nor do you want to become wedded to the idea of a particular cartridge for which rifles are made only by a handful of high-end gun makers at a very high price tag.

The beginning hunter will do best to stick with a handful of tried-and-true cartridges that are so widely used that they're likely to be on the shelves of American gun stores for the foreseeable future. Also, the more common a rifle cartridge is, the more selection you will find. For example, every major manufacturer of civilian ammunition produces ammunition for the .30-06. The .30-06, with a bullet of about .30 inch in diameter, has been around since the year 1906, first as a military round. It was picked up by civilians shortly thereafter and is now so ubiquitous that it's available in a wide selection of bullet weights and bullet designs, and varying charges of powder. Low-recoil, Magnum-loaded, or whatever you want (see Specialty Rounds, facing page) is made for the .30-06. Meanwhile, its brother-in-arms through two world wars, the .303 British, makes for just as good a deer cartridge, but most gun stores will stock only a single underloaded brand — if they have anything at all. (*Underloaded* simply means that the amount of powder will be well under what the cartridge is really capable of holding, with a corresponding loss of energy.) This is done sometimes for very old cartridge designs when manufacturers are concerned that early rifles chambered for them might be too weak to handle a full-power load: very nice for the person shooting an antique for fun, but not so nice when you are trying to put venison on the table.

As a beginning deer hunter, you would be wise to avoid buying a rifle chambered for either a very new or a very obscure cartridge. Every year there is a parade of new rifle cartridges trotted out by manufacturers and hobbyists. Some of these cartridges may eventually become accepted standards, but others never become popular, leaving the owners of those rifles without a reliable source for ammunition. There are easily over a hundred different cartridges that are appropriate for hunting deer. In practice, buying a rifle for such cartridges could lead to constant headaches and extra expense when purchasing ammo. I say this as someone who has a number of old rifles chambered for cartridges that fell out of favor more than a century ago. If you want to acquire such a rifle out of personal interest and a desire to take up old rifles as a hobby, then have at it. But if your goal is simply harvesting deer for food on a limited budget, consider opting for one of the common cartridges I describe below.

Specialty Rounds

If you start looking for specialty rounds for a common cartridge such as the .30-06 or the .308, you will find them.

Low-recoil loads will reduce felt recoil and give you about the same power out to a few hundred yards.

Magnum loads will get as much power out of a cartridge as possible, and you will feel it.

There are even **tracer rounds** with phosphorus dabbed onto the back of each bullet, which produces a laser-like streak of light along its path so you can see right where it went.

Three Kinds of Cartridges

B roadly, I would group the mainstream American deer cartridges into three categories. Any of them could do the job, but some will do better depending on the situation. As always, the bigger the boom, the more flexibility you have.

HIGH-POWERED CARTRIDGES

First, you have high-powered cartridges, which can be used to shoot deer from a wide variety of angles with full confidence of penetration (given proper aim), with the trade-off of moderate recoil. Among these are the .35 Whelen, the .30-06, and the .270 Winchester. The .270 is a modified version of the .30-06 case, which has the same powder capacity but the neck of the cartridge is narrowed to fit a .270 (7 mm) bullet, which weighs less than any .30 caliber bullet but has a flatter trajectory. The .35 Whelen is the .30-06 case necked up to accept a .35 caliber bullet and has a little more "boom" than most people need. While some people use it solely for deer, it is more often found among hunters who want to use one rifle for both deer and elk or moose.

MODERATELY POWERED CARTRIDGES

Then there are cartridges with not quite as much power as the .30-06, shooting bullets that usually don't weigh as much but still get the job done from most angles. The .308 Winchester is the most common among these and is available in almost as many varieties as is the .30-06. The 7 mm is a compromised version of the .308: almost as powerful but with less recoil and with a flatter trajectory with somewhat less energy delivered. The .30-30 is also in this category, although the shape of the .30-30 case is designed to work well in lever-action rifles, and there have been few bolt actions or semiautomatics made for the .30-30. The .280 is another midrange choice that many deer hunters in Vermont and New Hampshire swear by, usually chambered in the semiautomatic and pump-action rifles that those hunters have traditionally favored.

THE TERMS *RIMFIRE* AND *CENTERFIRE* refer to the primer that makes a cartridge go *bang* when the trigger is pressed.

A rimfire has the priming compound (which could be any chemical compound that explodes when pushed, such as fulminate of mercury) pressed into the rim of the cartridge. The firing pin of a rimfire cartridge needs to push against the rim of the cartridge base. A centerfire cartridge is detonated by a firing pin that pushes against the center of the cartridge base.

Most rimfires are less expensive to manufacture, but they don't provide a large or consistent enough ignition to use with larger bullets and volumes of powder.

LOW-POWERED CARTRIDGES

At the lowest end of the energy and recoil spectrum, the choices are relatively few. The .243 Winchester is small enough to be used on varmints such as prairie dogs and coyotes but still big enough for deer at the right distances. The 6.5 × 55 Swede is more effective than the .243 on deer, though it may be difficult to find in stores in the United States, in spite of being quite popular for other species of deer in northern Europe. There are smaller cartridges that will plausibly kill deer, but many states ban the use of any bullet smaller than .23 inch in diameter for the hunting of deer. The standard .22 LR rimfire cartridge that many people are familiar with is absolutely out of the question.

I have taken deer with many different cartridges and rifles and had the opportunity to evaluate their relative merits through experience and autopsy. The cartridge and the bullet really do matter. On average, I found that deer were running farther before death when I used mid-range types of cartridges. The difference between whether a deer runs for 30 seconds or 3 seconds before it realizes that it is dying is important. A deer can go a very long way in 30 seconds running flat out. When the deer's path takes it through thick brush (which it will almost inevitably head straight for), you might spend all day looking for that deer. I'm now using a .30-06 for the majority of my deer hunting. Since I made that switch, I have had probably 90 percent of my deer die either where they stood or within no more than 5 seconds of running.

I also often have shots presented that are as much as 200 yards away from me, which is a range at which the difference between a .30-06 and a .30-30 becomes very clear. If all my hunting was taking place in the short visibility of scrub pine, probably I would have chosen something a little lighter.

Common Deer Cartridges

Big Cartridges with Heavy Recoil

These can quickly kill deer from many angles, even at longer distances. They can also be used for larger prey, such as elk.

.30-06
.35 Whelen
.270 Winchester

Medium Cartridges with Moderate Recoil

These cartridges are perfect for deer, although they are not as flexible as some others.

.308 Winchester
30-30
7 mm-08

Small Cartridges with Light Recoil

These are as small as anyone should consider for deer. The .223 is not legal for deer in all states.

.223 Remington
.243 Winchester
6.5 × 55 Swedish Mauser

By now you're probably wondering what the story is with the names of all these different cartridges. The short answer is that there's no standard process for naming them. Some are indicated by a metric measurement, others in fractions of an inch. Even the nominal caliber may not have anything to do with the name. Sometimes the number indicates the diameter between the lands of the rifling and other times the diameter between the grooves. Sometimes a marketing department rounded the number up because it sounded better. For example, the .38 Special is not .38 inch in diameter, but rather .357 inch. It is not ".38" of anything (nor do I consider it particularly special). All cartridges seem to have numbers of some sort included in the name, but beyond that the name doesn't always tell you anything.

Bullets

Once you've chosen a cartridge, you'll have to give some consideration to the specific bullet loaded into it. Remember that the bullet is just one part of the cartridge, and you may find ammunition loaded with various types of bullets that may or may not be suitable for hunting deer. This is a separate issue from what the caliber or cartridge is. Different bullets are intended to do different things, ranging from punching holes in paper targets to hunting various types of animals.

soft point | soft point boat-tail | flat point for lever actions | polymer tip boat-tail | hollow-point handgun bullet

Here are a variety of common bullet designs, each intended for a different use.

SOFT-POINTED

Soft-pointed bullets can be used successfully for hunting deer and should be considered an ethical choice. These are lead bullets without a jacket. Sometimes there is a thin gilding of some other metal around part of the bullet, but nothing thick enough to function as a jacket. A standard soft-point bullet will expand as it hits the body of the deer, doing much more damage to the deer than an FMJ bullet, while penetrating farther and more reliably than a hollow-point.

PREMIUM

Then there are premium bullets. Many companies have designed patented hunting bullets with combinations of materials designed to offer the optimum expansion, penetration, and total damage done to the target. The difference in performance of premiums versus standard soft-points is real.

Many of these designs utilize a jacket of a carefully measured thickness that is open at the tip, where the lead interior is exposed. The open tip begins expanding as the bullet moves through the body of the deer, while the jacket limits that expansion to prevent the bullet from opening up too fast, slowing down, and failing to fully penetrate.

ALL COPPER. There is a new category of premium bullets today, made from 100 percent copper. They cost considerably more than standard bullets and ammunition, but they perform very well. To avoid the hazard of lead poisoning, hunters should consider using all-copper bullets if they intend to have venison as a primary, year-round source of meat or if they will be regularly feeding venison to a small child.

In 2008, the Minnesota Department of Natural Resources conducted a study in which the bodies of dead sheep were shot, then X-rayed and CT-scanned to determine the volume of lead fragments and their distance from the actual wound channel. The results were surprising: lead fragments were found up to 18 inches from the wound channels.

Trimming away the meat from within a few inches of the wound channel will be sufficient for the typical adult. Lead is a much bigger health issue for small children with developing brains, however. It doesn't take much to pose a serious risk to their health, especially if a child will be eating that meat on a regular basis. If you're concerned about the potential impact of lead on your health, consider hunting with all-copper bullets and using less-expensive kinds for your target practice.

SOME OF THE LEAST EXPENSIVE ammunition is also the least appropriate for hunting deer. Included among this group are full-metal-jacket (FMJ) bullets and hollow-pointed bullets.

FMJ. The purpose of FMJ bullets is to comply with international law by being able to punch a hole through something without doing any damage beyond the hole. A copper jacket covers the entire frontal area of the bullet; its purpose is to prevent the bullet from expanding or breaking up within the target.

Full-metal-jacket bullets were developed in the 1890s in response to bullets the British had developed, which expanded rapidly and broke up in the body. Other countries complained that the injuries were far more horrific than necessary to remove a soldier from combat. The issue was incorporated into the Hague Convention of 1899 and international law now effectively requires the use of full-metal-jacket bullets to limit the degree of injury.

FMJ bullets are relatively inexpensive to produce and can sometimes be quite accurate, but they are the opposite of what a deer hunter should hunt with. Your goal as a hunter is to try to kill the deer as quickly as possible, doing as much damage with one shot as possible. FMJ ammunition is usually cheaper than other types, but it is appropriate only for target practice.

Hollow-pointed. The tip of a hollow-pointed bullet has a hole in it that usually extends about a third into the bullet. The purpose of this is to shift the center of balance toward the back of the bullet while it is in flight. This design feature, in combination with other elements of bullet design, can make a bullet more stable in flight and enhance its accuracy.

Hollowing out the point of a bullet also affects what happens to it once it plows into the body of a deer. The bullet will expand rapidly to open into a doughnut shape. Generic hollow-point bullets will expand so quickly that the bullets fall apart. The result is likely to be a nasty wound, full of fragments of a bullet, yet not one that penetrates far enough to disrupt a vital organ. The deer may run a very long way, escaping the hunter entirely and dying of infection in a great deal of pain. Hollow-point bullets should be avoided among deer hunters for this reason.

Sighting Apparatus

Hunting rifles, muzzleloaders, and slug guns have two different types of sighting apparatus, occasionally both on the same rifle. Either way, you need to make sure that your sighting apparatus indicates the same point in space where the bullet or slug will impact the target. This is the whole point of having sights.

OPEN SIGHTS

First there are *open sights,* also sometimes referred to as *iron sights.* These are relatively simple pieces of metal attached to each end of the rifle. When the eye is properly aligned with them, a marksman familiar with that rifle can see where the bullet is going to strike. Sights are good for shorter ranges; with a little practice a hunter should be able to hit a target the size of a deer's lungs from within 50 yards. With very good sights and a whole lot of practice, some very talented people can hit targets consistently out to 300 yards.

SCOPES

Then there are scopes. A *scope* is essentially a special telescope that has been mounted to the top of the barrel. It has a *reticle* (sometimes referred to as *crosshairs*) permanently attached to the inside of one of the lenses. When the scope is properly adjusted for the distance from which you're shooting, the X marks the spot where the bullet will go. Once a scope has been properly adjusted and "zeroed," it is much easier to hit a target accurately than with iron sights. *Zeroing* refers to the process of adjusting sights so that they show exactly where the bullet will really impact the target.

It's important to properly mount and "zero" a scope before attempting to shoot a rifle at a living target.

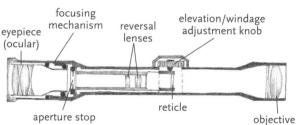

eyepiece (ocular) · focusing mechanism · reversal lenses · elevation/windage adjustment knob · aperture stop · reticle · objective

Most modern hunting rifles are sold with "clean" barrels: that is, there are no open sights and the owner is expected to select a scope to mount on it. Sometimes a new rifle will be sold as a package with a scope premounted, or you may be lucky enough to pick up a used one that comes with a scope. Most often, however, the choice of a scope is left to the buyer.

Once you've selected a scope, you'll need to purchase a base for it also, as well as the rings that attach the scope to the base. Although there are many different types of bases and rings for scopes (and some hunters have distinct preferences for or against certain ones), all you really need to do is make sure the base was made to fit your model of rifle and check that the diameter of the rings is the same as the diameter of the scope's body.

COST AND QUALITY. A scope can cost as much as you want it to. There are scopes that cost several thousand dollars, but there are also plenty of good "budget" scopes for under $100. (I am sorry to say that there are also plenty of really bad scopes out there for under $100.) The way to get the most bang for your buck on a cheap scope is to put your money into basic quality rather than added features. If you see an advertisement for a scope

Separately purchased rings and a base are usually required to attach a scope to the firearm.

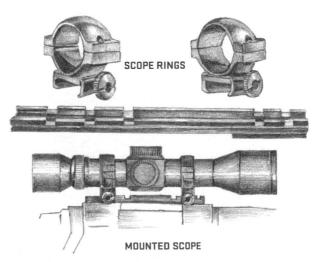

SCOPE RINGS

SCOPE RAIL/BASE

MOUNTED SCOPE

that costs $50 and has an illuminated reticle, zooms in to 24×, has an extra-wide 50-millimeter objective (the *objective* is the lens that is farther away from your face while looking through the scope), and promises all kinds of other whiz-bang features, stay away. For that price, they could not possibly have packed in all that technology and still maintained quality sufficient for dependable use.

On the other hand, if a manufacturer is offering a no-frills scope for $50 that focuses in the standard 3- to 9× range (or perhaps even a nonadjustable fixed-power scope) with an objective diameter of 32 mm or 40 mm, you are more likely to have something you can actually use in the field without worrying that the inside of the scope will fog up in bad weather or that the reticle will go out of alignment after each shot. On a low budget, the only features you want to be paying for are the various chemical coatings on the glass that do such things as reduce glare, enhance light transmission, limit fogging, and resist scratches.

Do not try to put a rimfire scope on a deer rifle. A scope made to work on a .22 LR rifle was not designed to withstand the recoil of a center-fire deer rifle. At best, it will go out of zero every time you fire the rifle. At worst, the recoil will destroy the scope.

While most gun stores sell used rifles, I have never been to one that sold used scopes unless they were attached to used rifles. If you have any friends who hunt or shoot targets, it may be worth asking whether they have some old scopes that you can have for free, buy cheap, or trade something for. You can also sometimes find used scopes for a low price on eBay. One especially good deal to look out for is when someone has bought a "package" rifle because it was on sale but didn't really want the scope and rings that came with it. He's got some sort of super-titanium quick-detaching rings that he insists on using with a $500 scope featuring German glass and some special reticle. So he gets the rifle home and immediately removes the brand-new scope and rings and lists them on eBay for whatever he can get. I have scoped several rifles with brand-new scopes and rings that I got off eBay or Gunbroker.com for as little as half the manufacturer's suggested retail price.

Unless you can round up a donation of parts from a fellow hunter, expect to pay at least $60 in total for the parts to scope your first deer rifle.

How to Install a Scope

Having acquired the parts, many people will then routinely pay a gunsmith $50 or so to actually install and align the scope. Feel free to use a gunsmith, but I think you are better off learning how to do this simple job yourself. It's sort of like knowing how to change a tire — it'll save you some money, and you never know when you might need to use the skill.

If you look at the top of your clean-barreled rifle, note how it has some little screws on either side of the top of the receiver that don't seem to do anything. All those screws do is fill the screw holes for the scope base temporarily, preventing dirt from getting into them. Different styles of base may use all or only some of the predrilled holes. Look at where the screw holes are on your scope base and remove those corresponding screws from the rifle. Use the screws that came with the base to attach it to the rifle.

First make sure you are using the right sort of screwdriver. Flathead screws on a gun have slots with straight interior sides rather than the slightly sloped sides of most screws. You will need to use a hollow-ground screwdriver to avoid buggering up the screw heads. Most interchangeable flathead bits (as opposed to the type that are permanently attached to the grip) tend to be hollow-ground. Newer rifles frequently seem to use hexagonal-headed screws that require a standard set of hex wrenches to remove.

Gunsmithing screws have a different profile from that of standard flathead screws.

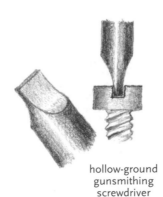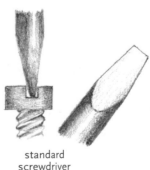

hollow-ground
gunsmithing
screwdriver

standard
screwdriver

ATTACHING THE BASE

Get that base good and tight — be firm with it. There are thread-locking compounds (one brand is Loctite) that you can apply to the threads to lock them in place, like glue for metal. You can find it at any hardware store for around $5 a tube. That's what a professional gunsmith would use to ensure a steady hold, but it's not the end of the world if you don't use it.

Follow the directions that came with the rings. If you got them used and there are no directions, you can look at the illustrations on page 77 to see how they usually go together.

Before fully tightening up the rings on the scope and base (and before applying any Loctite, since the clock starts ticking on you as it dries), shoulder the rifle and look through the scope. Is it at a comfortable distance for you? If it is too far away, the "eye relief" will be off and you won't be able to see the full image in the lens. If it is too close, either the image could disappear or you risk having the scope hit you in the face when the rifle recoils. Find a comfortable balance, moving either the rings along the base or the body of the scope through the rings to adjust the eye relief. Then either tighten up everything or mark the positions of the parts so you can take all the screws back out, apply your Loctite, and get it all back together the way you want it.

It looks like a proper hunting rifle now. But you aren't done, because the odds of that reticle just happening to point precisely where you need it are slim to none.

Those knobs along the body of the scope are called *turrets*. You will find that they unscrew easily. Underneath the removable caps are small dials; one of them moves the reticle from left to right and the other moves it up and down.

BORE-SIGHTING THE SCOPE

First you will want to *bore-sight* the scope. This saves time and ammunition in zeroing the scope, but it usually works only for bolt-actions (not lever-actions, semiautomatics, or many single-shots).

Unload the rifle and inspect the chamber to ensure that it is not loaded. If it has a magazine, remove it. Then take the bolt out of the rifle so you can look all the way through the rifle from the chamber end. Put the rifle on a *steady rest* in a place where you can see something that will serve as a virtual target at the distance you want to zero for. The steady rest can consist of a proper rifle rest or some sandbags, or a couple of bags of rice can stand in for sandbags in a pinch. The point is that the rifle will face forward and not move when you let go of it.

Your virtual target can be the top of a fence post, a distinctive flower, or anything small yet visible that you wouldn't mind having put a hole through if something went terribly wrong. It should preferably be roughly either 50 or 100 yards away. Adjust the position of the rifle on the rest while looking through the inside of the barrel until the virtual target can be seen right in the middle.

Now, being very careful not to move the whole rifle, starting clicking the dials on the turrets of the scope, each in turn, until the reticle is centered on that virtual target. Keep looking back through the barrel to make sure that the rifle has not moved slightly. When you can see the same point in the crosshairs as you see through the barrel, you have successfully bore-sighted the scope. Good work. Now put the caps back on the turrets and the bolt back into the rifle.

Sometimes you will get lucky and find that you've got the scope perfectly zeroed just by bore-sighting. More often, you will find that bore-sighting just gets you "on the paper" when you take the rifle out to actually shoot it at a paper target.

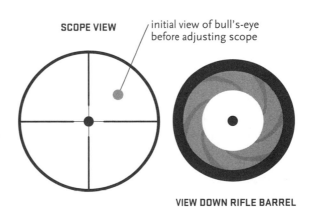

SCOPE VIEW

initial view of bull's-eye before adjusting scope

In this illustration, the target is high and right when seen through the scope, while the same target is centered when viewed through the barrel. To remedy this situation, the dials on the scope should be adjusted low and left.

VIEW DOWN RIFLE BARREL

ZEROING THE SCOPE

It is best to do the actual zeroing on a 100-yard rifle range, but with a
minimum of homework, you can get the job done at 50 yards if that is
the longest distance you have to shoot at. Few of us have a backyard that
offers 100-yard shots against a safe backstop, but if you live where it is
legal to shoot, you might find that you can set up an ad hoc 50-yard range.

You will need to set up a paper target with a clear bull's-eye. You
can buy paper targets at a gun store or you can just take a big piece of
paper (a full-size sheet of newspaper is a good size) and put a very visible
sticker or spot of paint in the middle.

Put your rifle on a nice steady rest again. Aim the reticle right at
that bull's-eye and shoot one round, being very careful not to jerk the rifle
or flinch. Then put on the safety, unload the rifle, and point the rifle in a
safe direction with the action open while you walk over to the target with
a ruler. If it hit the bull's-eye right away, you're in business (though you
should still fire a few more shots to confirm that it wasn't a fluke). If not,
measure exactly how many inches above or below the center of the bull's-
eye the bullet hole is. Then do the same for its position to the right or left
of the center.

The turrets of most scopes adjust point of aim by either ¼ or ½
inch. It will say which it is on the dial underneath the cap. For example, say
the bullet hole went 4 inches high and 2¾ inches to the left and your scope
adjusts in ¼-inch increments. In this case, you would turn the elevation dial
exactly 16 clicks down and turn the windage dial 11 clicks to the right. If you
get the directions wrong (some dials are poorly marked for this) and find you
have turned them the wrong way, this should be apparent as soon as you look
through the scope. No problem; you can just turn the dials back the other
way exactly the same number of clicks to get back to your starting point.

Get good and steady, then shoot again. If you've done everything
right, you will usually find that this second shot hits the bull's-eye pretty
squarely. If it is still off, put the safety back on and measure the distance
from the new hole to the center again. Repeat the process until you are
hitting the bull's-eye. It can't hurt to fire a few more shots after the first
bull's-eye, to confirm that you are really zeroed and that there isn't something loose that could cause the scope to go out of zero after the recoil of
one shot.

If you are zeroing at 50 yards but really want the thing to be just about dead-on at 100 yards, that should be pretty easy to do. At 100 yards most cartridges from barrels of between 20 and 24 inches will shoot within an inch of the point of impact they do at 50, so you can just zero the rifle to hit an inch high at 50 yards, knowing that it will be right on at 100. This method isn't precise enough to win any marksmanship contests, but you'll be close enough that it won't matter in terms of hitting the vital area on a deer.

Some scopes take knocking around better than others. The price you paid for the scope tends to figure into it. If you are on a hunting trip and drop the rifle out of a tree or something of that nature, it is quite possible that the scope is knocked out of zero. You are far better off in this situation if you have the know-how to rezero the scope yourself right away. Otherwise, either you have to end your trip and stop hunting until the gunsmith gets around to doing it for you (that could take months during hunting season when demand is high; good gunsmiths get really backed up) or you keep hunting with a rifle that might be out of zero and risk missing when the time comes. Or worse, what looked lined up to be a perfect kill turns out to be a deer shot in the guts and horribly wounded. You could spend all day and all night looking for that wounded deer because your scope was out of zero. It really does pay to know how to zero a scope on your own.

The Upshot

IF YOU FIND ALL THIS TALK of cartridges, ballistics, action types, and scopes to be hopelessly confusing, it's okay. You don't need to get too geeky about this stuff.

If you can't decide what to do, you can always just buy a bolt-action .308 that comes with a premounted scope.

Bow Hunting

Bow hunting is an approach best suited to advanced hunters and to people with a lot of spare time. There are a few potential advantages to bow hunting: Many states have special archery-only seasons; sometimes the archery season takes place during the rut, which is the best possible time to be hunting deer; and many hunters take up bow hunting for the sole purpose of getting in on the extra weeks of deer hunting.

There has also been a trend in some eastern states of establishing urban archery programs within areas that have a serious problem with deer overpopulation. Since there is rarely a safe direction to discharge a firearm while on the ground in a city, and because the sound of gunfire would result in a lot of 911 calls, these places allow deer to be hunted while limiting hunters to archery equipment. If you happen to live in such an area and you have deer in your backyard, it could make much more sense to buy a bow and hunt there than to buy a firearm and drive 30 miles to hunt.

Some municipalities make the legal ownership of even a hunting rifle so onerous that you may decide to purchase a bow for hunting simply because you don't have anywhere outside the city to store your weapon. In New York City it is possible to legally possess some types of hunting rifles, but the city requires that you spend a lot of time standing in lines, being fingerprinted, presenting letters attesting to the "good moral character" of the applicant, and so on. None of this is an issue if you hunt with a bow.

Many people have the impression that a bow is a silent weapon. This is not entirely true. It does not produce a sound with the same volume as a gunshot, but a bow still makes a twanging sound when the arrow is released. When a bullet is fired from a rifle, it is traveling faster than the speed of sound for at least the first few hundred yards. The result is that the bullet has either struck or missed the deer before the animal hears the shot. Not so with a slower-moving arrow. Deer can react and move so quickly that they "jump the string" at the sound of the twanging bowstring and move out of the path of the arrow before it reaches them.

RANGE

As hunting weapons, even the best bows in the hands of a typical archer are limited to about 40 yards (a traditional longbow could send an arrow much farther than that when shot into the air but was only effective as a military weapon against a massed body of troops, when no individual needed to be aimed at). It can take a long time to get that close to an animal in a place where you are allowed to hunt. The skill required to do this is admirable, but we should not assume that every hunter is making a game of the hunt. A bow is not the most efficient tool for putting meat on the table; you will probably have to spend a lot more time hunting. To some people, that reality is a problem, whereas to others, it is precisely what attracts them to archery.

Among those hunters who purchase a bow-hunting license in Virginia, only about a third typically tag a single deer all season. Bear in mind that bow hunters tend to be among the most knowledgeable and dedicated of deer hunters. They aren't buying the license just to sit at home. A member of a full-time hunter-gatherer society can survive as a bow hunter because he or she doesn't have much else to do. The full-time subsistence hunter doesn't need to show up at an office for nine hours a day or pay health insurance premiums. You probably do.

TYPES OF BOWS

There are several varieties of bows. A very small but dedicated group of hunters prefers the traditional European-style longbow, usually made from wood. These hunters may even make their own arrows from river cane and knap their own arrowheads from flint or obsidian.

RECURVE. Somewhat more common are those hunters who use a recurve bow. This type of bow has curved tips that increase the potential amount of energy stored. The recurve might sometimes be made of wood, but these days it will most often be made of some type of fiberglass or other composite material. A recurve bow can be strung for a higher weight than a longbow, resulting in greater velocities that extend the range and power of the weapon.

RECURVE BOW

COMPOUND BOW

Bow-hunting technology can vary widely, from the very simple recurve bow to the powerful compound bow.

COMPOUND. By far the majority of modern American bow hunters are using some type of compound bow. This bow is distinguished by a set of cams on each end that use the same principles of physics as a pulley or a block and tackle to allow the user to shoot a bow with a higher draw weight than they would otherwise be capable of. *Draw weight* refers to the amount of force required to pull back the bowstring. More draw weight means more potential energy to send an arrow flying faster and farther. Compound bows are always made out of a modern composite material such as fiberglass or carbon fiber, and they tend to cost about the same as rifles of similar quality.

CROSSBOW. Finally, we have the crossbow — essentially, just a regular bow turned sideways. It has a stopping device that allows the bow to remain drawn with the projectile ready to launch as soon as the trigger is pulled. The projectiles fired by a crossbow are called *bolts* rather than arrows, even though they look almost exactly the same. Crossbows are no more powerful than are compound bows.

There are two primary advantages of crossbows over other types of archery equipment (or *tackle,* as it is often called). First is that the ergonomics can be quite similar to those of a rifle. Someone who has a lot of experience with rifles may find that a crossbow is quicker to become competent with than a regular bow. Second, the hunter does not need to be able to hold the bow at full draw while waiting for the perfect shot. I have preferred crossbows during archery season because damaged tendons in both elbows prevent me from holding a bow at full draw for very long.

Not every state permits crossbows to be used during archery season. Check your local regulations, and don't assume that you can hunt with one. A new hunter should also be aware that there is a type of snobbery at work all through the archery world. Most serious archery enthusiasts consider crossbows to be a sort of aesthetic abomination. This is a big part of why some states prohibit their use during archery season for deer. Meanwhile, the people with recurve bows look down on hunters with compound bows as essentially cheaters. The guys with wooden longbows tend to look down on *everyone* else as impure. I suppose you get to do that if you're taking deer with arrowheads that you yourself chipped out of a piece of stone.

A modern crossbow mimics the ergonomics of a rifle, while offering about the same performance as a compound bow.

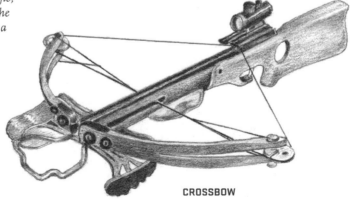

CROSSBOW

The Politics of Hunting

MANY PEOPLE have convinced themselves that they've rejected firearms out of some sophisticated understanding of how to protect society, when in fact the real reason is that many of them are from urban and suburban backgrounds and simply don't have any experience with guns. They tend to oppose private gun ownership because what they know about guns came from violent films and frightening news stories. It's as if we'd made up our minds about chain saws by watching horror movies and seeing lumberjacks stumble into the emergency room. Build a log cabin, and your opinion would likely change.

Many people reading this book may experience an aversion to the idea of acquiring and using a firearm. This fear is typically rooted in firearms being unfamiliar objects. If you didn't grow up around guns (I didn't so much as hold a .22 until I was 18 years old), then all your associations with them are almost by definition going to be negative; guns may have entered your consciousness only when you heard of a crime committed with one.

Having been a part-time subsistence hunter for the last 6 years, I no longer feel the same way about firearms that I used to. A majority of my personal context for firearms is now positive. They are tools that have fed my family. I have spent many a pleasant afternoon with friends shooting at clay targets or paper bull's-eyes. No sense of aggression or violence has ever accompanied my personal uses of firearms.

Practically speaking, if you are an adult of sound mind and without criminal intent, a rifle in your hands represents a danger similar to that of a circular saw. I own and use many power tools, and some of them scare the bejesus out of me. I am comfortable with circular saws; I must admit, however, that I have a pathological fear of chain saws. One false move, one unseen nail embedded in a piece of wood, and I could take off my leg and bleed to death. In my hands a chain saw scares me far more than a rifle does.

Many tools are potentially dangerous, so in the case of a circular saw or a chain saw or a rifle, we are obliged to learn how to operate these tools safely. That a tool is initially unfamiliar and scary does not justify running away from it. If that were the case, we would have no houses, airplanes, or automobiles. Things need to be built and maintained; potentially dangerous tools are required to do the work of the world. By all means, do these things as safely as possible, but do not allow the fear of something going wrong to prevent the work from being done.

Obviously, there are very good reasons for keeping all firearms away from violent criminals and the mentally ill. We have some excellent laws on the books to do that. We will continue to have policy debates about how to keep those people from buying guns, and there are some intelligent opinions on all sides. Provided that you are neither a violent criminal nor mentally ill, this debate does not need to have any bearing on your decision as to whether or not to purchase a deer rifle.

Being environmentally responsible is certainly consistent with both liberal and conservative values. The reduction of food miles and the reduction of your dependence on food that has its origins in petroleum-based fertilizer are examples of being environmentally responsible in your daily life. To this extent, hunting nonendangered animals for food is a reflection of modern environmental values.

When reduced to these terms, hunting for food becomes something very much apolitical. Long before anyone came up with any abstract ideas about how humans should interact and govern themselves in groups, we and the long parade of species that came before us were hunting and killing in order to feed ourselves and our young. The idea of hunting being politically controversial seems as strange to me as politicizing breathing.

Using a rifle to hunt for food does not have to mean that you identify yourself as pro-gun or antigun. It is a tool that we use to do a job, and it need not form the basis of a political identity any more than a chain saw does.

CHAPTER FIVE

TACTICS

At this point, it's likely that you have purchased or borrowed a deer rifle, have learned how to shoot it, and feel ready to go out hunting. The problem is that deer are not paper targets and will not do us the favor of standing still in prescribed places while we kneel and take aim for the perfect shot. The creatures will move about in vexing ways, managing to be where we are not with an alarming regularity. The only solution is to become skilled at knowing where they are likely to be at any given time, considering varying environmental conditions while also managing to escape their detection. Before any of that comes into play, however, it's a good idea to spend some time practicing your shot.

In Practice

When you practice shooting your weapon, you should be sure to try shooting in a seated, cross-legged position, standing, and while down on one knee. In field conditions, there is rarely a shooting rest presented for our convenience, so it pays to learn how to get your rifle steady without anything to rest it on. Dropping to one knee is a very quick way to get a steady shot at a deer that you see while standing up. While on one knee, you can rest your left elbow on the left knee (assuming that you are right-handed) and steady the fore end of the rifle. In the cross-legged position, the left elbow can rest on the leg in a similar fashion.

Sitting on the ground with your back to a tree offers a very stable shooting position.

When on foot, dropping to one knee quickly can help you get steady.

If a tree is handy, you may find that it helps you to get steadier than either off-the-knee or offhand.

Sometimes there is nothing to use for a steady rest and dropping to one knee is impractical. Shooting offhand may be your only option.

It is very easy to use the nice, comfortable shooting benches found at most shooting ranges and to forget to shoot in different positions. Practicing off a bench will not prepare you for shooting off-hand or while seated, and the moment a doe is in sight is not the best moment to start learning. Even if you feel ridiculous because everyone else is using a shooting bench, don't be afraid to get down in the dirt and shoot like a real hunter.

Outsmarting Deer

When you've had some time to practice and feel as though you're ready to head into the woods, there are a few key things to do to avoid making deer aware of your presence. Remember that deer have very good hearing and a keen sense of smell, and a fair sense of sight. Your goal, then, is to circumvent each of these senses.

SILENCE IS ESSENTIAL

First of all, be quiet. Do not make noise in the woods. Wear big, thick, clunky boots only if it really is freezing cold and you need to prevent frostbite. Otherwise, wear shoes or boots that you can walk quietly in. Some people who always stalk rather than ambush deer swear that going barefoot or wearing old tennis shoes makes the least amount of noise. American deer hunters traditionally wear heavy boots of some type, but it is worth noting that many of the old-time professional hunters in Africa who stalked elephant and Cape buffalo in the forest would wear very simple, light canvas shoes to move more quietly. American hunters probably developed the heavy-boot tradition because the deer season was always in cold weather for so long. As deer seasons have been changed to start earlier and earlier in some places, it doesn't make sense to wear the same heavy boots in the heat of the early season.

Choose all your fabrics carefully, including that for your daypack, and leave behind any that may make noise. Many synthetic fabrics make a loud *zip* sound when the slightest little twig slides against them. Even some jackets and packs made in woodland camouflage patterns will make this noise, so don't assume that it's a silent material just because it seems to be marketed to hunters.

Don't carry loose change in your pockets. It may clink at the worst possible moment. Bring some tissues, so you aren't constantly sniffing while you're out in the chilly air. Any piece of equipment carried on your belt or in your pockets that tends to clink should be deadened somehow; a monopod clipped onto the belt can easily tap against a knife or hatchet while you're walking. Consider putting metal objects into separate pockets or perhaps wrapping a strip of duct tape around each item.

Do not fidget more than necessary while sitting in ambush. If you'll be hunting from the ground in the woods in a concealed position, you may want to push the dried leaves away from the spot where you'll be sitting, in order to avoid rustling them.

Turn off your cell phone. Setting it on vibrate may not be good enough. How many times have you faintly heard someone else's cell phone vibrating in his pocket from across a room? If you can hear it, a deer can definitely hear it and will recognize it as an artificial noise that doesn't belong in the woods.

Be mindful of the noise your rifle's safety lever or button makes. The safety of a brand-new rifle in particular will tend to produce a loud *click* when switched on or off. This click can be heard by a deer from an amazing distance. Some safeties can be silenced by putting a little bit of electrical tape at the spot where the edge of the lever hits another piece of metal. Experiment with your own model on a rifle range to make sure that this will not prevent the safety from working properly. If nothing else, at least be aware that this sound is going to happen so that you know to wait until the right moment to flip off the safety. That right moment could be when there is some other natural noise to mask it, or perhaps when you are fairly confident that the deer is not close enough at the moment to hear it.

STAYING DOWNWIND

Preventing a deer from hearing you is simply a matter of adopting certain habits. Keeping it from smelling you comes down to one thing — the wind. Always know which way the wind is blowing. Always. When you get out of the car or step out of your back door, the first thing you should be doing is testing the wind. If it's very cold, exhale and watch where your breath goes. Licking your finger and holding it up works well enough most of the time. If the movement of the air is very light, you could carry a little baggie of fine ash or talcum powder and sprinkle a pinch in the air to see which way it moves.

The wind blows your scent to anything that is downwind of you. Animals can smell only that which is upwind of them. If there's a particular area where you're expecting to find deer — in a stand of acorn-laden oak trees, for example — you should always try to approach that area while remaining downwind from it. This can require traveling in a wide and inconvenient circle, but it's worth it.

If you see some deer 150 yards off and you realize that they're downwind and there's a very slight breeze, get steady and prepare to shoot right away (assuming you're in a good position and can consistently make a clean shot at that distance). It takes time for that scent to blow over to

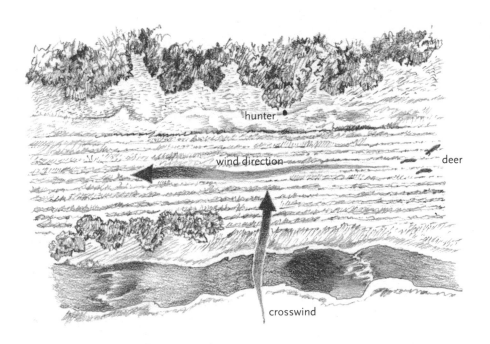

Always try to position yourself downwind of the deer.

WORKING THE WIND will serve you well, and you don't really *need* to do anything except that. But there is another option — scent control.

Deer hunters are employing scent control more often now than ever before. I will warn you, though, that it is a lot of work, and it is very expensive to go for complete scent elimination. It can't hurt to do the minimum, which is to avoid using any perfumed hygienic products on the day of your hunt. Buy scent-free soap and also use it in place of shampoo if you don't have scent-free shampoo (which can be hard to find). Wash your hunting clothes with scent-free detergent. If you can't find scent-free detergent, just wash them on a hot cycle with a cup of baking soda in place of the detergent. The addition of a cup of borax will reduce odor even further. Try not to work up a sweat, which necessarily produces odor, when you're hunting.

To go beyond this, you can purchase special scent-controlling hunting clothes made from materials engineered to trap or neutralize scent particles. Such an outfit, including socks and perhaps boots, can cost hundreds of dollars. The people who use this gear will often put on the clothes only once they are in the woods, keeping them sealed in plastic bags otherwise, to prevent household scents from affecting them. There are also scent-killing sprays and cover scents that can be used while hunting.

But that is really postgraduate hunting technology. The beginning locavore hunter does not need to master any of the more advanced scent-killing technology to hunt for food. Mostly, it's for hunters who are seeking out very old and experienced bucks that are extremely difficult to see in the wild, let alone manage to shoot. When any random doe will do to put meat on the table, you probably don't even need to think about advanced scent control. Just mind the wind, and you'll get a deer.

The beginning hunter does not need to utilize advanced scent-killing technology in order to hunt for food.

the deer. You have a matter of anywhere from a few seconds to perhaps a full minute before they get wind of you, depending on how fast the wind is moving. It is possible to beat the wind and make a good shot before they sniff the air and run.

When stalking (or *still-hunting*, as it is counterintuitively called), always hunt into the wind. Crosswind (sideways to the wind) is also acceptable. If you set up a blind or an ambush, always try to face into the wind. Deer may very well show up behind your position, but you probably won't get a good shot at them anyway, since they will have scented you and run away. Facing downwind would mean that you'll only see in a direction that deer will avoid on account of your odor.

ELIMINATING VISUAL DISTRACTIONS

The best way to avoid catching a deer's eye is to stay still and wear the right clothes. As you may recall, they don't see very well into the red end of the spectrum. The blaze orange that deer hunters are usually required by law to wear for safety purposes is visible to a deer only as another shade of gray. Blaze orange in a camouflage pattern is probably better than just a solid mass of orange; it stands to reason that a big human-shaped blob of a single shade of light gray is going to stand out against a background of many intermingled shades.

If you're going to wear camouflage, choose a pattern that matches the landscape of the area you're hunting at the time you're hunting it. If you are expecting to have snow on the ground during deer season, then dark green camo with oak leaves printed on it probably would not hide you as well as would a pattern with patches of white. But if you can't afford to spend the money on a new outfit, it isn't essential. If you go with earth tones — dark khaki, hunter green, tan — you will be camouflaged enough to have some success. Just stay still, and you should blend in adequately. There are still a lot of unsophisticated deer out there for you to eat.

DITCH THE WHITE AND BLUE. What you really don't want to wear is anything white or blue. A flash of white might be mistaken by another hunter for the movement of a deer's white tail. (Though no hunter has any business shooting at the back end of a deer in the first place, it's best not to tempt fate.) And remember that deer see into the blue end of the color spectrum quite well — possibly better than we do. Do not wear blue jeans or a blue denim jacket. Wearing blue will make you immediately obvious to the deer, even out of the corner of its eye.

AVOID FANCY DETERGENTS. Modern laundry detergents advertise that they can brighten colors, which is true. They do this through the use of UV-reflective dyes. Deer can see into the ultraviolet spectrum, so use of normal detergent effectively makes your clothes glow to the eyes of a deer. To avoid this it's best to wash your hunting clothes in a detergent that does not contain all those advanced dyes and scents that most others use. Many stores that carry hunting gear will stock this type of detergent as hunting season approaches.

Finding Deer

Having a fair idea now about how to escape detection *by* deer, we turn to the detection *of* deer. Where are they at a given time, and how do you catch up with them? Bear in mind that there are specific dates within which deer can legally be hunted on any land with a given weapon. The dates of these seasons vary widely from place to place. Exceptions may sometimes be granted by special permit to farmers suffering heavy crop depredation.

In most of North America, whitetails feed heavily on acorns, apples, and beech nuts during the autumn. Different species of oak trees will drop differing volumes of acorns at different times. Get to know what kind of oaks or other important food sources are in your area and when they tend to drop their nuts or fruits. Depending on the species, a single mature oak tree in a good year can produce up to 600 pounds of acorns. That is a major source of food.

When the acorns are dropping (usually in late September through the end of October), find the oak trees in your hunting area and wait for the deer. Depending on your budget and personal preference, you can either set up a tree stand or a ground blind to conceal yourself or just find some natural cover to hide behind, and stay very still.

Tree Stands

SHOULD YOU SET UP a tree stand for hunting? This can expand your field of view and allow safe, downward shots in flat country. But it also costs money (starting at around $50 for a real cheapie) and has its own set of risks and disadvantages.

Using a tree stand requires the purchase of the stand, a safety harness, and some type of ladder with which to get up into the stand. This setup is inherently immobile. If you want to have the option of moving to a more productive spot when you haven't seen any deer all day, you'll need to have tree stands set up in a variety of hunting spots. Hunting from the ground enables you to get up and move to another spot at will, without dropping hundreds of dollars on multiple tree stands.

Also consider that a majority of accidents and deaths suffered while hunting deer are caused by hunters falling out of tree stands. Climbing down the side of a tree, in cold weather with slightly numb hands and feet, perhaps in the dark, is not an entirely safe thing to be in the habit of doing, particularly with a firearm. In my own case, I know myself too well. Eventually, I'd get impatient, cut corners, and find myself not bothering with the harness, putting myself at risk of breaking my neck in the middle of the woods with nobody to help me. And what if you are prone to falling asleep while sitting on the stand? It's a question of knowing yourself and managing your risks accordingly.

I don't bother using tree stands. I've had very good luck seeking out a hillside to sit on.

Often, I can find some tall grass or brush to get behind. For me, this is also more comfortable than being strapped to the side of a tree on a tiny metal bench for hours on end. The choice is really up to you, though.

POSITIONING

Consider your positioning carefully, minding the direction of the wind. When hunting with a rifle, you don't usually want to set up a tree stand or a blind right there within the oak grove; it's too easy for the deer to notice you before you have a good shot opportunity. Set yourself back at least 50 yards. Look at roughly where you are expecting the deer to be standing.

Is there a safe backstop? You mustn't shoot at a deer silhouetted against the sky because there's no telling where the bullet will end up. Don't fire your weapon unless you can see for certain where your bullet, slug, or arrow will stop, even if you miss by a bit. Usually, this means having the bullet strike the earth where you can see it. This is accomplished either by shooting downward from an elevated position (such as a tree stand) or by taking advantage of undulations in the landscape. For example, if a deer is standing on the downward slope of a hill, you could probably take that shot. If the bullet goes all the way through the deer, it will impact the side of the hill and do no harm to unseen people or property. If that same deer is standing on the very top of the hill with the sky behind it, you should wait until it's in a safer spot. On flat land all of the same rules apply; it's just harder to set up a good shot. An elevated tree stand can help to open up more shot opportunities in flat country by enabling you to shoot downward.

HOW DEER APPROACH THEIR FOOD

When you choose your position, think about how deer are likely to approach their food source. They like to travel either in cover or close to it. For this reason, it makes sense to pay attention to fence lines when evaluating an area to hunt in. When the landscape consists of small patches of woods and brush intermingled with farmland and perhaps housing developments, fence lines become the hidden highways of the local deer population. Wherever you have a fence that is mown up to but is not regularly cleared of brush, a line of trees will grow up alongside it. Eventually, the vegetation will tend to widen, and deer will create a path within its cover. Watch the fence line, and you will eventually see deer.

If there is an overgrown fence line extending close to a stand of oak trees, the deer will travel along that fence line to reach the acorns under the oaks. In this case, you definitely want to avoid using that very fence line as cover. Otherwise, if you're facing the oak trees, hunkered down near the fence, the deer are likely to come up right behind you and bolt before you even know they're there.

When hunting a tree line, try to position yourself (●)
off the direct path that deer (★) are likely to travel.

STEADYING THE RIFLE

Consider how you are going to get steady for your shot while in your place of ambush. It's a good idea to either buy or make a simple monopod to shoot from. Find a strong Y-shaped stick (or cut a properly shaped green branch from a tree) to put in the ground and rest the fore end of your rifle on. Decide whether you intend to sit on the ground or in a portable chair while shooting, and determine the overall length on that basis. A commercially made monopod (or bipod or tripod or whatever you want to use) will usually be adjustable to different heights.

In the interest of being less encumbered while traveling to and from my hunting spots, I have found it very handy to purchase a cheap carabiner-style key chain and attach it to my commercially made monopod. I unscrew the yoke to place the ring of the key chain around the top of the stick, then screw the yoke back in. I wrap the metal of the carabiner clip with camouflage-patterned duct tape (regular duct tape will work fine if it isn't too shiny) in order to prevent it from clinking against anything and making noise. Then I can put that clip on a belt loop, where it can be instantly grabbed and set up if I suddenly see a deer while creeping through the woods.

Rigging a monopod with a belt clip is simple to do.

THE WAITING GAME

Odds are that you will be doing a lot of waiting. It can be boring or meditative, depending on your personality. I have found that hunting a good stand of oaks while the acorns are on the ground is usually interesting even when the deer haven't shown up yet. Squirrels, black bears, and wild turkeys all eat a lot of acorns, and depending on what is in your area, you may see any of these animals. Squirrels in particular will help keep you awake and alert. A squirrel hopping and rustling around in the leaves sounds very much like a deer taking cautious steps. This happens again and again while you're sitting there, and every time you hear it, you'll think it's a deer and spend a second or two thinking that you're about to have a shot.

When hunting in the woods (as opposed to fields) with dry, crunchy leaves on the ground, I have found that I can take a book along with no real danger of missing a deer. It is impossible for even a deer to move silently in that situation. I can put down the book invisibly and shoulder the rifle while I'm in the ground blind I've constructed. But this option of passing the time with a book is out of the question when there is snow on the ground or if the dead leaves are wet (and therefore silent) from recent rain. Nor is it a good idea to have your eyes on a book when hunting a field or the edge of a field: you won't hear an animal that approaches in the grass.

The use of an MP3 player or similar device with headphones is totally out of the question. You need your ears to be working for you at all times. Even if a deer isn't headed your way, someone walking through the woods might be calling out to you to make sure you know he or she isn't a deer.

PEAK HUNTING TIMES

A failure to see any deer after hours of waiting is not necessarily a sign that you should pack up and go home. A deer could show up at any moment. But if you don't think you're up to sitting there all day long or if you just don't have the time, there are peak hours during which you can concentrate your hunting.

DAWN AND DUSK. Radio-collar studies of deer have confirmed that during legal hunting hours (there are precious few places where one can hunt at night), deer are most active around dawn and dusk. The first two hours after dawn and the last hour before dark are the hours of peak movement for whitetails overall. There are always going to be some individuals that have different habits and could be out there walking past your stand at one in the afternoon, but most deer activity is concentrated around dawn and dusk, so those are the times when you really need to be out there.

Those peak hours of movement are part of the reason it is always better to practice many short hunts at the end of the day than a few all-day hunts. Not only are you hunting at the most productive times, but being out there in the same places again and again will teach you the natural rhythms of the habitat as well. The same rabbit may run from a brush pile to the long grass 15 minutes before dark every day. The squirrels may take a last few jogs up and down their trees. You'll come to understand the normal routines of nature in that very spot, and it will make you a better hunter; you'll know right away when something has changed and from which direction a deer is likely to emerge. If your employer will allow it, try to arrive at work an hour early and leave an hour early during hunting season so you can be in your blind before the sun goes down. Even if you've only got 30 minutes of light left, you'll be out at the best time. That habit is better than using a full day of vacation time.

Alternatively, you could hunt every morning before work. That's effective up to a point. That point will be when you have a deer on the ground that needs gutting and processing and you realize that you need to be at work in 45 minutes.

WEATHER-RELATED MOVEMENTS

Probably through a physiological response to changing air pressure, deer move around a lot and spend more time than usual seeking out food in advance of cold weather or a snowstorm. Remember that a deer has a rumen, and it can accommodate a few days' worth of food in there. This way it can bed down in thick cover and try to wait out the bad weather as comfortably as possible. So watch the weather: If the barometer is dropping and there is a storm front predicted to come in the next morning, see if you can leave work a little early to get out there and hunt right away.

There is typically a corresponding increase in deer movement immediately after a storm has blown through as well. When the weather has been stormy for a few days, the deer are likely to be hungry and especially eager to start moving in search of food.

Hunting immediately after a big blizzard is an experience not to be missed. The deer are moving, and their footprints are clearly visible in the fresh snow. The snow (unless it is iced over) will silence your footsteps. With the wind in your favor, you may even be able to follow a particular set of tracks through the woods and fields and catch up with the deer. Proceed carefully, constantly scanning as far ahead as possible to ensure that you see a deer before it sees you. Deer typically bed down facing the wind. This means that by minding the wind, you have a chance of coming up behind a deer and getting off a shot before it knows you are there. Older and wiser deer may know to double back on their tracks in a wide loop so that anything following their tracks must necessarily approach from upwind.

HUNTING DURING THE RUT

During the rut, you'll just need to be out there as much as you possibly can. For those two weeks or so of peak rutting activity, there is so much deer movement all the time that you have a very good chance of seeing deer at any time of day. Their normal sense of priorities and timing go right out the window, as both males and females move in search of a mate.

Hunting the rut allows the hunter a special set of very effective tactics that don't work at other times. Does make a particular sort of bleating sound when they are in estrus. There are tube-shaped calls that can be purchased to imitate that sound and attract bucks. Hunters can also purchase urine from farmed estrous does (or synthetic scent, if farmed urine is not allowed to be sold in your state). A splash of this doe urine can bring in bucks from downwind.

You could also try using a pair of shed or fake antlers. Click them together to simulate the sound of a pair of bucks fighting. This is called *rattling*. Rattling attracts bucks that hear the sound and think two bucks are fighting over a doe. It usually brings in two types of deer. First, you have the young and inexperienced bucks. They haven't quite figured out yet that they are nobodies in deer society during the rut. If they get into a fight with just about any buck, that other buck is probably stronger and more experienced and will thrash them soundly. They run in there because they don't know any better.

The other deer that tend to respond to rattling are the most dominant bucks. They've been winning their fights so far in the season, and they assume that they'll be able to intimidate or defeat whatever bucks they hear fighting over the next hill. Most of the deer in between these two extremes know better than to go rushing into a fight that they might lose. Bucks get injured during these fights, and sometimes they will even be killed.

The only downside to the deceptive tactics used during the rut is that they will tend to attract bucks rather than does. In most parts of North America, we are facing a problem of deer overpopulation. The best way to address that problem is by hunting more does than bucks: Shooting a doe prevents her from dropping a pair of fawns the next spring. Killing one doe effectively reduces the population by at least three for the following year, whereas killing one buck reduces the population by only one. Whatever doe he might have impregnated if he had lived will almost certainly find another buck to do the job, unless the doe-to-buck ratio has become so skewed that the remaining local bucks can't get around to all the does before they go out of estrus.

Hunting on a Small Property

I f you are hunting a small parcel of land, you will often be forced to make do with a less than ideal hunting situation. On my own property of 6 acres, there are only a few safe directions to shoot. I have few mature oaks, no reliable water source, and not much in the way of food for deer. One would expect that this would make for difficult hunting, yet I manage to take deer regularly.

Even if there is nothing on your property to hold the attention of deer for long, the key is just getting them to walk by and stop long enough for a shot. In my case, I realized that there is a large area of very thick cover on the property behind my house, as well as 40 acres of pasture on the horse farm across the street. This means that many deer will bed down in the thick cover to sleep, then commute over to the big pasture to nibble on clover. My opportunity was in the commute.

Close inspection of the ground for tracks and deer scat showed that the deer were traveling between these two areas along an old overgrown fence line at the edge of my land. The problem was that this fence line had grown up to about 15 feet across. Mature hardwoods are in the center of it, right up against the old barbed wire. Then there is a screen of blackberry brambles and other brush on either side. The deer were traveling through the middle of this in what amounted to a tunnel that I couldn't see inside of to shoot.

The solution was to mow a path through the meadow on my side of the fence line. I did this in the spring and maintained it for a few months. I placed a salt lick along the path to attract the attention of the deer. It wasn't long before they had switched to using the path that I had made. Deer are lazy and found that this clear path was easier to use than the old one, which had fallen branches and tree trunks blocking the way at intervals. Once they had gotten used to it, I didn't even need the salt lick any more (it was gone by the time hunting season started).

They've been using this path for about three years now. I keep the grass in that meadow high, mowing only about once a year to keep back the brush. The tall grass next to the path gives them a sense of security with the fence-line brush on their other side. I am able to sit about 50 yards away and shoot a deer as it passes. Shots on moving deer are not for beginners. However, they will usually pause for a moment to nibble on something along the way, and I take my shot very quickly at that moment. It is also possible to get them to stop briefly.

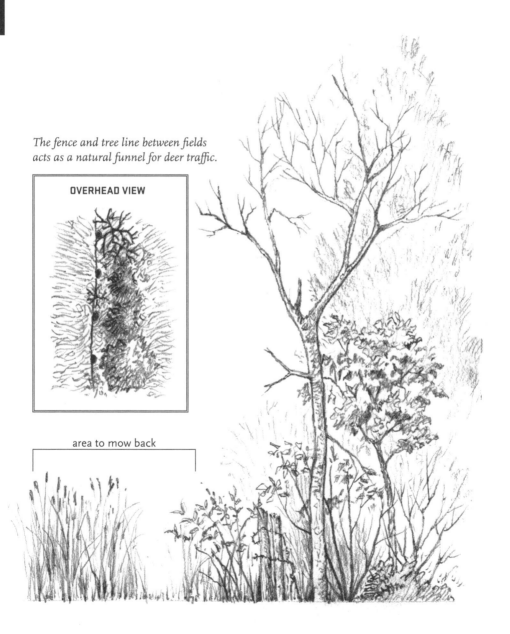

The fence and tree line between fields acts as a natural funnel for deer traffic.

OVERHEAD VIEW

area to mow back

FUNNELING DEER TRAFFIC

This structure I manipulated is known as a *funnel* in deer habitat. When you find yourself limited to a small piece of land to hunt on or if you're hunting later in the season, when deer are feeding on browse in a scattered way, it's a good idea to seek out or create such a funnel. Look at a satellite map and identify the bedding areas of thick cover, then look for sources of water and food. Draw lines between these points while keeping them close to the kind of cover whitetails prefer. Examine the topography along those lines you have drawn. Look for a spot where you can set up a good, safe shot that isn't directed toward a road or a house. That is going to be a very good place to look for deer.

Other features that can function as a funnel are a mountain pass, a wadeable area along an otherwise deep river, and a gap in a fence. Passes and fords across rivers and creeks aren't the sort of thing you can go creating on your own, but a funnel can be made by deliberately removing a section of fence or placing a log or rock on an old barbed-wire fence to press the wire against the ground. (Don't go taking apart people's fences without asking first.) Even if a deer is physically capable of jumping over a fence, it would probably rather not go to the trouble. You or I also might be able to climb over a fence, but if there's a gate nearby, we're likely to use it, right?

When you find yourself in a situation where a deer is probably going to be walking past you without having a reason to stop, you can usually buy yourself at least a few seconds with a stable target. Blowing into a grunt call (a plastic tube that produces a sound like that of a buck grunting), even ineptly, will cause a walking deer to stop and look around to see where the other deer is. You'll probably not have more than 5 seconds to shoot, which is more than enough time if you were already steady with your rifle in position. If you don't have a grunt call, there are plenty of other noises that can work. Any animal sound will arouse a deer's curiosity. Even yelling "Hey, deer!" will result in the deer stopping for a few seconds to look around before bolting. A few seconds could be all you need.

Scouting

The day that you hunt should not be the first time you visit the land you'll be hunting on. Satellite maps can help you size up an area before hunting, but they can't completely take the place of being out there on foot to see where the deer and their food sources are. Regular visits to your intended hunting ground will help you understand the area better.

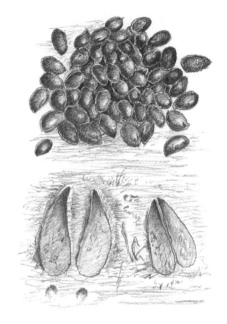

Deer scat and footprints are easy to identify. The relative freshness of either is an indicator of how recently a deer has passed by.

Scouting can be enjoyable and is comparable to the proverbial day at the park. Pack a picnic; bring a camera and binoculars. As you walk around, look carefully for footprints, scat, and any other evidence of deer. You might be able to identify bedding areas, which will be oval-shaped depressions in tall grass or bush with scat and cloven footprints nearby. Pay attention to what types of trees you see. Oak trees are going to drop acorns that are an important source of food for deer when hunting season starts. Any regularly mown grass or hayfield will also serve as a food source and gathering area in the fall and winter. Try walking along the edges of any fields to look for deer trails where deer will be entering the area.

Once you have identified food sources and travel routes that deer in the area are using, start looking for good sites where you can hide or set up a tree stand from which to ambush deer. As you're looking for ambush positions, remember to consider how far you've proved yourself capable of making an accurate shot with your chosen weapon. It's best not to set up too close to where the deer will be if you can help it, but don't put yourself so far away that you're likely to botch the shot.

SHOT PLACEMENT

You find yourself in the perfect position. By studying maps, you've identified a great deer funnel and set up a ground blind or tree stand with a perfect view of the deer that has just stepped out from the woods and is now calmly grazing in a field. There's a safe backstop with a hill behind it, and you're ready to take the shot.

Where to Aim

Which part of the deer do you aim for? "The front end," some would answer. Okay, that's true, but it's not specific enough. A deer can be killed very quickly by shutting down either the nervous system or the cardiovascular system. Stopping the cardiopulmonary system is probably the more common approach, accomplished by a shot through the lungs, the heart, or the arteries that connect to the top of the heart.

CARDIOPULMONARY ORGANS

The lungs present an excellent target because they are about the size of a football in their broadside outline. You don't need to be a fantastic shot to hit that with a rifle from a long distance, and it leaves a lot of room for error when aiming for the center of the lungs.

The heart, below the lungs, is a much smaller target of roughly 3 inches by 5 inches in profile on a smallish deer. Usually, smart hunters will aim for the lungs, and if they happen to hit the heart, they will smile and silently take credit for making a challenging heart shot when in fact it was purely an accident. Hitting just above and slightly forward of the heart will kill the deer even more quickly than will a shot to the heart. An injured heart may still be pumping some blood briefly, though at a reduced capacity. If a bullet severs the thick blood vessels that connect it, the blood pressure drops to zero more or less instantly. The heart has been totally disconnected in that case.

THE NERVOUS SYSTEM

The nervous system presents a tempting target, though a difficult one. A bullet through the brain will absolutely drop the deer instantly like the proverbial ton of bricks. Yet a deer's brain is a very small thing. Most of the volume of a deer's head consists of sinuses and mouth. Aiming for the whole head won't do the job. If you flub that shot, the deer will suffer a very slow and horrible death. It may be unable to eat or drink with a blasted-apart jaw. Consider that the part of a deer that is most often in motion is the head. The head is the part most likely to move at the very last second, when it's too late to stop the trigger pull. Head shots are an advanced tactic that I feel should not be considered by beginners. I won't say that there's never a place for them, but it takes a very keen understanding of the rhythms of a deer's movement, a solid grasp of the anatomy of the head, and well-placed confidence in your ability to make that shot from whatever position you find yourself in.

THE SPINE SHOT. There is another way to turn most of the nervous system to the virtual "off" position — shooting through the spine. A spine shot is tricky but definitely less risky than a head shot. Pay close attention to the anatomy, and you'll see that the spinal cord isn't exactly where you might expect. It is not right under the skin, but rather 4 or 5 inches beneath the surface of the skin over the shoulder. The spine right over the shoulder is actually wider in profile than a deer's brain is.

This shot provides more room for error than a head shot. If you are a bit low, you still hit the lungs. A bit far forward or backward, and you'll still hit the spine. Too high, and you will have inflicted a nonfatal wound to the deer, which will surely be painful but from which it will probably make a full recovery.

A good spine shot should hit just over the lungs, increasing the odds of a clean kill.

When done properly, a "high-shoulder" shot to the spine can destroy the top of the lungs at the same time. This depends on your elevation and the particular bullet you are using. It may be worth mastering this shot if you are hunting on a small parcel of land surrounded by property owners who will refuse to allow you to step even a few feet onto their land to retrieve the deer. I have been a victim of this sort of pigheaded refusal, and it was heartbreaking to watch vultures circle around my deer while my refrigerator was empty. If this could be a problem for you, then you have a special need to ensure that the deer you shoot does not take another step after you pull the trigger. Shutting down the nervous system is a more effective means of guaranteeing this than is shutting down the cardiopulmonary system.

Every now and then a hunter will get lucky and find that an errant shot has still hit an artery, resulting in swift death. Theoretically, it is possible to kill a deer with even a shot to the leg. In practice, it is not possible to aim for most arteries. They present such narrow targets and are so difficult to locate from a distance on the outside of the body that it is not practical to shoot one deliberately. A shot to the neck has exceptionally good odds of disrupting an artery, but there are still many spots on the neck that would not result in a swift kill. Like the head, the neck is in motion more than the rest of the body, and it would be very easy to flub the shot.

THE FIVE POSITIONS

Not only are there specific organs that need to be penetrated, but also the point on the deer's hide that you aim at is going to vary based on how it is standing relative to you. There are five basic positions that the deer may be presenting to you.

STANDING BROADSIDE is the ideal scenario. A deer standing broadside provides the hunter with the minimum depth of flesh and bone to penetrate before hitting the heart or lungs, while also being a simple silhouette over which to visualize the positions of the organs.

QUARTERING TOWARD the hunter is an acceptable shot, depending on your particular weapon and the distance between you and the deer. There is more to penetrate on the way into the lungs, but you've still got a little room for error. With the "boiler room" up front, your odds of hitting only organs that are slowly fatal (rather than instantly so) are minimal.

FACING TOWARD you is an advanced and iffy shot at best. The outline of a deer's lungs from head-on is a much smaller circle than that seen from the side. With this smaller target, you must be an accomplished shot and quite sure of your aim, or you should not take it.

A. *standing broadside* B. *quartering away*
C. *quartering toward* D. *head-on*
E. *the "Texas heart shot"*

QUARTERING AWAY means that most of what you have in front of you is really the digestive system. If the deer is steeply quartering away, you will have to send the bullet through the rumen and stomach to reach the heart and lungs. This means that you will have a bit of an extra mess on your hands when you are gutting it. Worse, if you flub the shot or if your bullet lacks enough energy to fully penetrate that many inches of flesh, you might wind up with a gut-shot deer. A shot through any part of the digestive system will absolutely, positively kill that deer. The problem is that in the absence of any other serious injury, it will take between 2 and 12 hours for death to occur. During that time the deer will still be mobile, and you probably won't be able to catch up to it, meaning that you will have to hang back and despise yourself until the time is up. For this reason, don't take a quartering-away shot at all unless you know for certain that your bullet is up to the job, that your aim is true, and that your grasp of the anatomy is correct.

FACING AWAY is really the last thing you want to see. Also called the Texas heart shot, this position should be passed up in all but the most desperate of situation and even then should be attempted only with a rifle/cartridge/bullet combination that you can be completely sure is capable of around 3 feet of penetration through flesh and perhaps bone. For example, a .30-06 loaded with a Winchester Silvertip bullet, fired from 30 yards away, would almost certainly reach the lungs from that angle. A .30-30 probably would not, and that same .30-06 bullet could fail to do the job at 100 yards. Bear in mind that you will probably damage one or both of the hindquarters in the course of this and lose quite a lot of meat. The best course of action is not to shoot at a deer in this position.

Usually, it is best to wait for the deer to present a good standing broadside shot. If the deer appears comfortable, isn't aware of your presence, and is in no hurry, then you shouldn't be either. It'll move around, and you'll eventually get a better shot on it. The time when I would suggest risking a trickier shot presentation (assuming that your firearm and shooting are up to the task) is when something is forcing you to act quickly. All things considered, a beginner will do best to stick to a standing broadside shot to the lungs, to end the deer's life as quickly as possible.

Things That Go Wrong

Aside from poor shooting, there are a few things that most commonly contribute to a shot's hitting the wrong part of the deer or missing it altogether. You'd think that once you've steadied yourself and have a good shot on a deer that's standing perfectly still at a reasonable distance, there'd be no way to miss. Unfortunately, that's not the case (trust me — I know). In these situations, it helps to know what can go wrong and how to make the best of things.

The late, great professional hunter Peter Capstick told a story in his classic book *Death in the Long Grass* about a client hunting in Africa who made a mistake so bizarre that I can only relate it in Capstick's own words:

> I told the gentleman to please place a large hole in [the lion] with all dispatch, and he got into shooting position. Five times he worked the bolt of his .338 custom Mauser, but the lion did not fall. In fact, he hardly hurried his stately exit after a disdainful glance at us. My client was doing everything right except for one minor item: he had forgotten to pull the trigger. As the saying goes, I kid you not. He was *positive* he was firing the rifle, in fact, became furious with me when I told him he had merely worked the bolt of the action. Only when I picked up the unfired cartridges and gave them back to him did he believe me. In the excitement he was positive he was actually shooting at the lion, and to this day I suspect he wonders if I pulled some sort of practical joke.

SHORT-STROKING

I have never been guilty of that one myself, but then again if I was, I probably wouldn't admit it. What I have done is something similar, called *short-stroking* a bolt. Short-stroking is when you flip up the bolt of a bolt-action rifle and pull it back as you should but fail to pull the bolt all the way backward before slamming it back home and locking it down. If the bolt does not come back all the way, the bolt face does not reach the edge of the top cartridge of the magazine and thus cannot carry it into the chamber. When you pull the trigger, you will find that nothing goes *bang*.

The cause of short-stroking is usually the shooter's having done a lot of practice with a rifle that had a shorter bolt throw than the one that he is using to hunt with. A .22 bolt action is an almost indispensable means of getting in a lot of target shooting without spending very much money. But watch out for the difference in length between the bolt of the .22 rifle and the bolt of your deer rifle. If your hands are accustomed to pulling back a bolt only 3 inches before pushing it back, that's probably what they will do in a stressful situation.

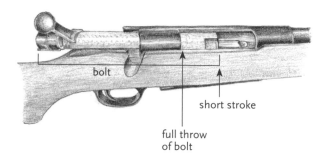

bolt

short stroke

full throw
of bolt

"Short-stroking" a rifle's bolt means failing to pull it back completely.

BUCK FEVER

When you're in position and have the deer in your sights, you might find that your hands are shaking too much to take what should be an easy shot. This phenomenon is called *buck fever,* and it is a bit difficult to explain. Everything may have been fine up to that point: you've found a good spot and a deer has appeared within range. But suddenly you find that you just can't get steady. Your hands are shaking, and you might even be hyperventilating; the "fight or flight" mechanism has kicked in, complete with a surge of adrenaline.

AN OBSTRUCTED SHOT

Shooting through brush or branches of any kind can be real trouble. When a bullet clips a branch, its course changes slightly. At close range this might not matter. An experiment with shooting through wooden dowels with a target about 10 yards behind the dowels demonstrated that bullets will veer off course by as much as 4½ inches across those 10 yards. Extrapolating that variance across 50 yards from branch to deer

FOR YEARS I smugly asserted that I had never been the victim of buck fever. Every time I'd put a deer in my sights or scope, I'd remained perfectly calm and done the job coolly.

I had always made a point of selecting a doe to shoot. Around midsummer I had been seeing a few mature bucks that were really exceptional animals. I had always told myself that all I cared about was the meat and that shooting a buck rather than a doe meant nothing. But watching these bucks got my imagination going. They were difficult to get close to and observe and they had large, majestic antlers.

One afternoon, early in the season, I was hidden on a bluff overlooking a power line right-of-way. One of the bucks I had seen earlier in the year stepped out of the woods with its back to me. I looked at it, amazed — it was about 70 yards away. At first there was no good shot. Then he reared up to eat some leaves from a branch, and that was when I got a good look at the antlers.

I'm not supposed to care about antlers. I'm a meat hunter. Yet somehow they affected me. I watched the buck through the scope as he browsed. Finally, he shuffled around and presented me with a perfect broadside shot. This should be easy. Only 70 yards with a scoped .30-06 and a broadside shot. Textbook perfect.

My hands trembled, my breathing increased, and my heart raced. I got as steady as I could and fired.

The deer ran away, unharmed. I had missed an easy shot on the best deer I had ever seen. I walked to the spot where the deer had been when I fired to confirm that there was no blood. I found where the bullet had hit the ground, having passed about 4 inches under the buck's belly.

Boy, did I feel stupid.

I shouldn't have taken the shot when I did. It would have been better to hold off and focus on getting my breathing under control. That miss could have just as easily been a bad shot that wounded the deer.

There were two things that I did right that day. One of them was not giving up. Don't think a missed shot means all the deer are scared off and it's time to go home. As a matter of fact, I walked right back to the same ambush spot and no more than 15 minutes later a couple of does came by, and I got one of them. The more important thing, though, was to make sure I really did miss the first shot.

shows that the bullet would be off from its correct point of aim by about 22 inches. If you were lucky, that would just be a miss that went right past the deer. If you were not so lucky, that could be the difference between a heart shot and a bullet that plows through the abdomen, with all the misery that such a shot entails.

It is important to be sure that the path between you and the deer is clear of any such material. Of course, in thick woods, where you may stumble across a deer that is only 15 yards away, deflection by brush would be a more acceptable risk than it is over a 100-yard shot.

A CLEAN BARREL

Another cause of shots gone wrong is, perversely, a scrupulously clean barrel. Think about it: when you calibrated your scope, all but one shot was from a fouled barrel. A bullet will behave slightly differently on its way out of a squeaky-clean, oiled barrel than it will as it comes out of a barrel with some fouling in it from previous shots. The point of aim through that scope was by definition adjusted to the behavior of bullets shot from a fouled barrel. But if you cleaned and oiled your barrel between your last session of shooting and your hunt, the very first shot you fire (presumably at a deer) will go slightly in a direction you don't expect.

THE FOULING SHOT. For this reason, it is advisable to fire a *fouling shot* before hunting. This ensures that the first shot of the hunt will land where you expect it to. In a modern, smokeless-powder firearm, there is no danger that the barrel will rust out or become corroded from the fouling of a single shot sitting in the barrel for a few days or weeks. Consistency is the key to accurate shooting. Change anything to do with the barrel, and you will probably change where the bullet lands.

AN UNSTEADY HAND

Mind *how* you get steady prior to the shot. If the barrel of your rifle is resting directly on a hard surface, such as a boulder, a tree trunk, or a stone wall, it will have a tendency to jump away from that hard surface as the bullet is traveling through it. Naturally, this will tend to throw the bullet a little higher than you'd wanted it to go. You can still use a hard surface as a rifle rest, but you need to put something soft between it and the barrel or fore end of the stock. In a pinch, your hand will do (the one not squeezing the trigger). You can also use your hat or remove a glove or grab any other soft object that's handy.

A MOVING DEER

Taking a shot at a deer while it is moving can result in a miss or a bad shot. I won't say that you should never do this, since I have successfully taken several deer while they were walking. But it is an advanced type of shot. There are two ways of dealing with this situation to get off a good shot.

DISTRACTING THE DEER. First, you can try to get the deer to stop moving by blowing into a grunt tube or making some other deerlike sound. The deer, being by nature a social animal, will stop for a moment and look around for the other deer. The catch is that it will probably be looking straight at you, the source of the sound. You will have anywhere from 2 to 10 seconds to squeeze the trigger before the deer runs off, so be ready to shoot right away when you blow that grunt call. It isn't a large window of opportunity, but it should be enough to make the shot.

USING A SHOTGUN. The other way of successfully making a shot on a walking deer without just horribly wounding it is to practice shooting moving targets with a shotgun. This isn't for everyone. Each year I shoot about 600 clay pigeons with a shotgun. That's not many, compared to serious shotgunners, but it's enough to build and maintain some skill at tracking a moving object in space and swinging a firearm just right to make lead intersect with it. (Busting clays also happens to be a lot of fun.) I wouldn't dare try shooting at a *running* deer with a rifle, but if it's moving at an easy walk, I can swing just a bit ahead of where I intend to hit and drop the deer pretty well.

CHAPTER SEVEN

AFTER THE SHOT

O nce you learn the craft of hunting deer, the hunt itself becomes relatively easy. Unless you're hunting in a new area, finding and shooting a nontrophy deer for meat is mostly a matter of being patient and attentive. Eventually, you'll find that you've internalized many tactics to the point that you implement them almost unconsciously. The real work begins after the trigger has been squeezed.

The Follow-up Shot

Whether you're hunting with a rifle, a shotgun, or a bow, you should immediately reacquire the deer in your sights and ready another shot without the slightest hesitation. You should be familiar enough with your weapon that you can do this without looking away from the deer. Even if you're hunting with a single-shot rifle, there's no reason you can't have another cartridge ready in a sleeve on the stock or between the knuckles of the hand that holds the fore end of the rifle. Don't think about whether you need another shot before chambering the next round. Thinking takes time, and a second or two spent in consideration of this could be the difference between whether or not the deer gets up and runs into the woods while you're still preparing to shoot again.

If the deer is actually in the process of getting back onto its feet, there is a real possibility that the bullet will not have hit an immediately vital area, and the animal could run a very long way before collapsing. In this event, you must shoot again, even if a good shot is not presented. Normally, you wouldn't pull the trigger unless you have a clear shot at a vital area. When you have a deer that's already wounded, though, the rules change. A vital follow-up shot would be preferred, but really, you should just shoot at whatever part of the deer you possibly can at that point. Anything you can do to get it on the ground (or perhaps get lucky and hit an artery) should be done.

Preparing for the Follow-up Shot

AFTER I'VE TAKEN A SHOT, my hand automatically works the bolt of the rifle, chambering a fresh cartridge. Emerging from the recoil, I must immediately reacquire the deer in my scope in case a follow-up shot is needed. In theory, I keep shooting as long as the deer is on its feet, or if it is down and looks to be getting back up. In practice, this is rarely required, but one should be prepared anyway. In most cases, the deer has either bolted straight into the nearest brush, where it collapses within 50 yards or so, or it drops on the spot.

WHEN THE DEER IS DOWN

When the deer drops within sight and you can see that it lies still, your job will be much easier. Go ahead and wait for a minute or two with the scope or sights still leveled at the body, just in case. Sometimes a shot that goes just above the spine can damage one of the dorsal projections of the vertebrae without actually breaking the spine. This shocks the deer and drops it only temporarily. It looks just like a true spine shot and an instant kill, with the important distinction that the deer will suddenly spring to its feet after up to a minute on the ground, then run away. Be ready for this by keeping the crosshairs on the deer and the safety of the rifle switched off until you are sure the deer is really dead.

WHEN THE DEER RUNS OFF

Should the deer run out of sight after the shot, you'll need to keep a cool head and resist the inevitable temptation to go running after it. Do not stand up or do anything to reveal your presence. The deer does not necessarily have any idea where you are. A gunshot will boom and echo, and it is often difficult to pinpoint exactly where the sound came from. In fact, the deer may not have the slightest idea what happened and may not even know that there is a hunter to be worried about.

In case the deer has not yet succumbed to its wounds, you must not do anything that will give it the sense that it is being pursued by a predator. A deer that thinks it is being chased will run farther and harder. Even a deer that has only a minute to live might manage to run a very long way before succumbing to blood loss or organ failure. In 60 seconds a deer can run far enough through woods and heavy brush that it'll take you the next 8 hours to find it. A wounded deer that does not sense pursuit will usually stop running and bed down in whatever cover is handy. There it will die in relatively close proximity to the hunter, making recovery of the meat much simpler.

Because of the great importance of this, when the deer runs *out of sight* after the shot you should wait at least 10 minutes before moving from your position. During that time, it is crucial that you take careful note of exactly where the deer was standing when you shot it. Also note exactly where it ran and at what specific point it disappeared into cover.

Think about how the deer behaved after being shot and replay that in your mind. All of this will be useful if you have to track the deer.

EVIDENCE OF THE HIT. After about 10 minutes, you should flip the safety back on and walk quietly and carefully to the exact spot where the deer was standing when it was hit. Sometimes the evidence at the scene will be immediately apparent. Sometimes you'll even see the dead deer once you reach the point where it started from. There are those rare times, however, when it becomes necessary to get down on your hands and knees and start looking for evidence.

Evidence of what? First of all, evidence that you really did hit the deer. This usually comes in the form of blood, hair, or other tissue on the ground. Having established that the deer was hit, you need to examine all available clues to determine what part of the deer you shot. The particulars of the shot will determine the likely amount of time until the deer dies of its injuries, and thus the amount of time you'll have to wait before tracking it.

This search for evidence needs to happen even if you don't think you hit the deer. If the trigger was pulled in the general direction of a deer, initially you need to work under the assumption that the deer has been hit. Every time you shoot at a deer, go and look for signs of a hit. The only exception to this is if you clearly see something like pieces of bark flying off a tree trunk next to the deer.

It's a horrible feeling to imagine a wounded animal out there dying slowly. In this rare situation, the ethical hunter wants nothing more than to immediately end the suffering of the deer. But if that deer is still capable of getting up and running, then tracking it too soon is likely to have the effect of scaring it off, pushing it farther and farther away and reducing the chances of recovering it at all.

Tracking

There are three primary things that you'll start looking for at the site of the hit: hair, blood, and tissue. Every time a bullet or a broadhead arrow hits a deer, it clips hair on its way in. There will *always* be some amount of clipped hair after a hit. Blood does not necessarily reach the ground right away, so it may not be evident at the scene. Bits of bone and tissue may end up on the ground as well, but that's usually the case only when there is an exit wound. Whether there is an exit wound depends on what kind of cartridge you're using, the distance of the shot, and the construction of the bullet.

HAIR

Careful inspection of the hair found at the scene of the shot may reveal roughly where the bullet entered. Deer are not just a uniform gray in color; different parts of a deer's body are covered with hair of slightly different shades and textures. Usually, there is not much hair on the ground, and it will tend to be a sprinkling rather than large clumps. If the deer was standing with shrubs or trees directly behind it at the moment of the shot, try looking up off the ground for any hair that might have been clipped from an exit wound. You will rarely find hair at a quick glance. There is usually so little of it that a really careful examination will be required.

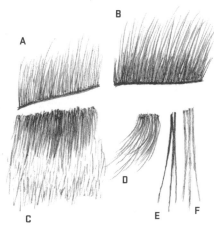

Hairs from different parts of a deer have different color and texture. **A.** *summer coat* **B.** *winter coat* **C.** *flank to white belly hair* **D.** *brisket* **E.** *back* **F.** *body*

BLOOD

There is usually some blood, and the color of it can tell you a great deal.

PULMONARY. Pinkish, frothy blood indicates a lung shot. A deer shot through both lungs will be dead within 100 yards. In this case, you do not need to wait more than 20 minutes from the time of the shot before trailing it — 20 minutes is the longest that a double-lung-shot deer could possibly manage to live, even if the lungs were only grazed. Usually, a deer with such a wound will die much faster than that. Of the deer that I have shot through the lungs, I have observed them to run no more than 30 yards. Several of those deer dropped in their tracks and appeared to die instantly, possibly due to being in a state of calm and having just exhaled before being shot. Again, because a lung-shot deer is going to die on its own in short order, it should not be tracked until that 20 minutes has elapsed. Do not force it to run while it is still able to.

ARTERIAL. A very bright (but not pink) crimson usually indicates arterial blood. This is one of the rare exceptions that call for immediate pursuit. A deer with a severed artery, assuming that no other major organs are destroyed, will die of massive blood loss. The question is how quickly. By immediately pursuing it, you have the chance of surprising the deer, if it is still alive, and causing it to run.

Running increases the deer's heart rate and causes it to lose blood even faster. A running deer with an open artery will probably cover less ground before dying than will a walking deer with the same injury. Serious bleeding is less likely to clot and stop flowing if the deer has to keep moving. Forcing it to run in this situation will also tend to produce a blood trail that is easy to follow.

MUSCULAR. Blood of the ordinary red color, neither especially bright nor especially dark, is an indicator of a shot through muscle. Think of the color of blood that you see after pricking your finger. Bear in mind that a shot through muscle may also pass through other organs, so keep looking for more clues that there has been more damage. If all signs point to only a muscle hit, you might recover the deer but shouldn't keep your hopes too high. A good-faith effort should be made after waiting about

20 minutes and then treating it like an arterial hit. It could be that you got lucky and nicked something more vital, but the blood from that part of the wound channel just wasn't reaching the ground for you to see it. A broken bone might also slow down the animal after the first 50 yards or so. Between a broken bone, gradual blood loss, and shock, you have some chance of wearing down a deer with a hit in a nonvital area by steadily pursuing it and jumping it again and again until you can get off another shot at it.

ABDOMINAL. Darkly colored blood is what you really don't want to encounter. Dark blood, which may have some particulate matter suspended in it, indicates an abdominal wound. If it is so dark as to be almost black, you are looking at an intestinal wound, which could take up to 8 hours to kill the deer and in exceptional circumstances as long as 12 hours. Blood that is somewhat redder than that indicates a shot to the stomach, which will result in death within no more than 4 hours.

The liver of a deer is found in the abdominal cavity, partially fused to the rumen and right behind the diaphragm, which separates the digestive system from the heart and lungs. A shot to the liver will result in death within 2 hours and can be diagnosed in part by the almost maroon color of blood that tends to be found on the ground within a few dozen yards of the site of the hit. The liver is often hit accidentally while you are trying for a lung shot. Odds of recovering such a deer are excellent, as long as you wait 2 hours before following it up.

For your own sake, as well as that of the deer, which will have to suffer horribly if you make this error, please do your best not to shoot a deer in the abdomen.

Sometimes a gut-shot deer will die faster if other organs or arteries have been disrupted. For example, if the deer was quartering somewhat steeply away from you and your rifle is capable of great penetration, your bullet would pass through the digestive system before hitting the heart and lung area. If you see evidence of both a gut shot *and* pink, frothy blood or particles of lung tissue, time your pursuit for a lung-shot deer and wait no more than 20 minutes before tracking it.

127

TRACKING

NO BLOOD AT ALL. Even a fatal shot doesn't always result in blood on the ground, especially if there isn't an exit wound. Shots that enter higher on a deer's body tend to produce less initial blood. Consider that the blood must flow down the side of the body and that the hair may soak up some of this blood. If the deer runs right away, the blood trail might start some distance from where the deer was hit. A blood trail might also stop after some distance if the opening of the wound becomes clogged with tissue or, in the case of an abdominal wound, partially digested food. In such cases, the internal bleeding generally continues but the blood trail becomes less visible.

BEHAVIOR AFTER THE SHOT

The deer's behavior after the shot may tell you something as well. A healthy deer will run off with its tail flagging. Sometimes a wounded deer will do that as well, but a deer that tucks its tail between its legs is definitely hit. Similarly, running on three legs or with a pronounced limp obviously indicates a hit. Note that a deer running on three legs might also be hit in a more vital area than just the leg; a bullet can pass easily through the shoulder on its way into the lungs. Deer seem to move along quite fast for a while on three legs, so under no circumstances should you allow yourself to believe that it will slow down enough on three legs to enable you to immediately outsprint the animal in the woods.

FOLLOWING THE TRAIL

Once you have waited the prescribed amount of time, you can begin tracking. It is helpful to have another person along for a tracking expedition, especially if there is any chance of the deer's still being alive. You can either track or hunt, but you can't exactly do both at the same time. If your eyes are on the ground and watching for drops of blood, you might not see the deer standing 30 yards away until it has bounded off.

BLOOD. Follow the drops of blood, being careful to walk *next* to the blood trail rather than right on it. You never know whether you will have to double back or start over for some reason, in which case it would not do to have stepped on or kicked over leaves with blood on them. If you are ever in doubt as to which way the deer was going, you can look closely at individual splatters of blood. The points on each drop are like arrows that point in the direction in which the deer was moving when the blood fell. They will appear only on one side after falling from something in motion. If you see drops that have a symmetrical splattering, that indicates the deer was standing still at that spot.

As you follow the blood trail, you may find it useful to mark the trail with bits of toilet paper, which are visible from far away and can help to visualize the direction that the deer could be headed. It is biodegradable if you don't manage to pick up every piece later on; and having some toilet paper with you in the woods is a pretty good idea for the more traditional reason, anyway.

Blood spatters are like tiny arrows pointing in the direction the wounded deer was traveling.

Tracking a Wounded Deer

HOW LONG SHOULD YOU WAIT until following up on a deer after diagnosing the likely injuries?

Spine/brain: 0 minute
Muscle: 0–20 minutes
Arterial shot: 20 minutes

Heart shot: 20 minutes
Lung shot: 20 minutes
Neck: 20 minutes
Liver shot: 2 hours
Stomach shot: 4 hours
Intestinal shot: 8–12 hours

DISTURBED GROUND. Deer do not usually run at top speed through the woods. They normally walk, which doesn't leave much of a trail. When a deer runs flat out away from a predator, it tends to kick up an obvious trail of overturned leaves that can be followed. This will be more or less evident, depending on what else has been moving around in that area of forest and how damp the leaves are. But sometimes you'll luck out with a very obvious trail of kicked-up leaves to follow straight to the dead deer.

If you shot at one deer among a group that all ran into the woods together, it can be difficult to figure out which one you hit. In the event this happens and you don't have a good blood trail, remember that a wounded deer will quickly separate from the rest of its group. Because of this, you can find the point where a trail of kicked-up leaves separates from the larger trail and — this is most likely the path to your prey.

PARALLEL TRAILS. You may see what appears to be a pair of parallel blood trails running through the woods. This happens when there is an exit wound and blood is dripping from both sides of the deer.

VOLUME OF BLOOD. In no case should you ever try to make a judgment about the deer's situation based on the total volume of blood that you see on the ground. Deer can die quickly despite leaving barely a drop in evidence, and they can also lose up to a third of their total volume of blood (or up to 2 liters) before dying. That's a lot of blood pooled on the ground along the trail, but it would be very difficult to calculate whether it amounts to one-third of the blood volume of a deer you haven't weighed.

The good news is that needing to track a wounded deer is the exception rather than the rule. If every hunt involved leaving the deer in the woods for 8 hours before even starting to track it, very few people would hunt. If you have prepared properly for the hunt by learning to shoot well and by studying the anatomy of the deer, your targeted deer will usually be dead within a minute of the shot. You can improve your chances by not taking a shot at a deer that is farther away than you have consistently made in practice and by taking care to get steady for your shot.

CHAPTER EIGHT

OKAY, IT'S DOWN: NOW WHAT?

T he real work usually starts after a deer is down. Even an experienced hunter may well sigh at this point, because the relative fun of going for a walk in the woods and trying to predict where deer will be is over. From this point on it's all work. The new hunter will find that after an initial sadness at the death of the animal and elation at a successful hunt, the sense of responsibility for an unfamiliar task is almost overwhelming. Don't worry — everything is going to be okay. You'll have some work ahead of you, but there are some simple instructions you can follow to ensure that this situation results in venison for dinner.

Making Sure It's Dead

Once you've got the deer on the ground, make sure it's actually dead before you approach it. This is especially important if you're dealing with a long-antlered buck, which could put an antler tine through your rib cage if you make the mistake of getting too close.

A dead deer will have open, unblinking eyes. Closed eyes mean that the deer is almost certainly still alive. Often the tongue is out after death. This should be evident even from 3 or 4 yards away. Obviously, the deer will not be moving if it is really dead. If you get close and find that there is still some slight motion, make your own judgment on what to do based on how long it has been there and where the wound appears to be. If the deer was shot an hour previously, by all means finish it off right away. You can tell for certain if the deer is dead by approaching away from the legs and antlers and touching the open eye with the end of the barrel of your rifle. If the eye does not move, then the deer is definitely dead.

If the deer is not dead but you can see for certain that the injury will be quickly fatal, one option is to wait quietly at a respectful distance while the deer finishes its death. I prefer to do this if it has been only a short time (perhaps a few minutes) since the shot; so soon after being shot, I figure, the deer is likely to be in shock and not yet experiencing pain. I feel that the deer is entitled to that last minute of fading away in relative peace, and I will give it a finishing shot only if the animal appears to be struggling or taking a long time to die.

WHEN ANOTHER SHOT IS NEEDED

If you do find that the deer needs another shot to finish it off, think carefully about where you put that bullet and about how close to the deer you are standing.

If the deer is down for the count, take the time to consider carefully the angle and presentation of a coup shot. Consider any damage that could occur to the meat. You may want to take a few steps in a direction that will allow you to slip a bullet into or just above the heart from behind the shoulder rather than directly through it (since the shoulder represents a meaningful quantity of edible meat). If the deer's head and neck are not in motion, a shot to the brain can be very effective. Do not place the muzzle of the weapon directly against the body of the deer or you will likely get splattered.

I have had several experiences in which this process went horribly wrong. I once came upon the scene of a car accident in which a Volvo station wagon had collided with a yearling buck. The humans were unharmed, the car was totaled, and the mortally injured deer lay kicking weakly at the air. Fortunately, I had a rifle in my trunk, which I could use to put the deer out of its misery. Since we were in a rural area, nobody else on the scene had a problem with that.

Standing no more than 2 or 3 feet away, I aimed the rifle directly at the deer's heart with the muzzle only about 6 inches away and squeezed the trigger. First there was a simultaneous bang and a hollow sort of thump from the animal's chest. This was quickly followed by both the sound and the sensation of tiny bits of *something* raining down on me. I realized with horror that I was covered by a mixture of gory deer bits and dirt that had gone flying up in a geyser and come down right onto me. The rubberneckers applauded. The moral of the story is that it is definitely possible to get *too* close for a shot with a high-powered rifle.

Slitting the throat of the downed prey is a cliché most of us have heard, but I do not suggest this course of action unless you are out of ammunition. In the first place, it requires getting too close to the antlers or hooves, which could suddenly kick with a renewed strength. In the second place, it is surprisingly difficult to slash quickly through the skin of a deer's neck, let alone get deep enough to sever an artery. The skin is stronger and tougher than one would imagine. Starting an incision is more difficult than continuing one that has already been opened. At the very least, you will need an extremely sharp knife to make an efficient job of it.

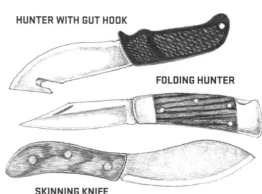

HUNTER WITH GUT HOOK

FOLDING HUNTER

SKINNING KNIFE

There are a number of knife designs that are practical for use with deer.

Field Dressing

O nce you have determined that the deer is dead, the mission shifts to preserving your meat. The first goal is to cool down the meat as quickly as possible. Gutting (which is synonymous with the term *field dressing*) is the fastest way to cool down the whole deer. Gutting also lightens the deer's body considerably, making it easier to transport out of the field. The only situation in which gutting isn't necessary is when you're actually quartering the animal in the field and leaving most of the carcass behind (see page 139).

CHOOSING THE RIGHT KNIFE

The most important tool for gutting is a very sharp knife — sharper than you may be in the habit of keeping your regular pocketknife. There are a wide variety of knives available for this purpose. Most of them can do the job, but some work better than others. The best option is a fixed-blade (nonfolding) knife with a 3- or 4-inch-long blade. It should be somewhat broad in order to work well for skinning.

Other knives have definite disadvantages. Folding knives tend to get a lot of fat, tissue, and coagulated blood jammed into the crevices of the grip, which makes it difficult to clean and fold up out in the field. Very large knives are difficult to maneuver carefully and make it too easy to cut deeper than you intended, resulting in unnecessary slashes through the hindquarters that interfere with really fine butchering work later on. A knife that is too big can also be dangerous while gutting, as that makes it easier to slice your other hand while you are reaching up into the dark of the abdominal cavity.

THE GUT HOOK. A gut hook is a handy feature on a hunting knife, though not strictly necessary to do good work. The purpose of a gut hook is to lengthen an incision at a carefully controlled depth. To this end, the hook is sharpened on the inside curve and typically has a blunt end. The gut hook has all manner of other uses, such as opening a box without potentially damaging the contents.

MAKING THE INCISION

Begin with an incision from the top of the sternum (breastbone). Slip the tip of your knife through the skin, down to the bone. In as smooth and continuous a motion as possible, continue the incision along the center of the underside of the deer. When you get past the breastbone and reach the abdomen, be very careful not to cut too deep. You want to cut down to the small intestines *without cutting them open*. If you accidentally open them up, you can deal with it, but the smell and mess are awful. The worst-case scenario is that you have to wash some digestive matter off the meat. Using a gut hook helps avoid cutting too deep and keeps the blade out of the guts.

Keep bringing that incision back toward the rear end of the deer until you get close to the genitals. At this point, stop and make two other incisions that fork off like a Y. Those two branches of the Y will go around either side of the genitals and up above the anus, where they will meet just underneath the tail. Using a length of twine or string, tie off the bung.

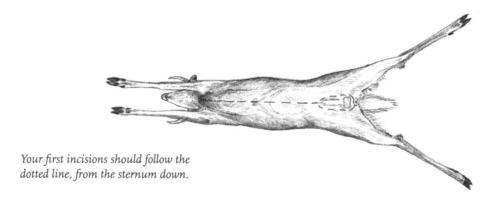

Your first incisions should follow the dotted line, from the sternum down.

CRACKING THE STERNUM

Digestive organs will start spilling out a bit at this point, but you'll have an easier time emptying the upper chest cavity if you crack open the sternum area. To do this, either break the sternum itself or pop off the ribs on one side where they meet the sternum. On a very young deer, this bone is not fully ossified and can be cut fairly easily with a knife. With an older deer, it will take a little more effort to pry or cut this area apart. On older deer with stronger bones, I have found that it is much easier to cut through the ribs just along one side of the sternum.

Up to this point, you've probably done a good job of keeping your hands clean. There is remarkably little blood at this stage of the process, unless the deer experienced a lot of internal bleeding or your shot was a bit too far back and went into the abdominal cavity. Now, though, things start to get messy.

REMOVING THE ORGANS

With the skin on the belly of the deer opened up, you can see how all the internal organs are held in place or connected to one another. Start working around the inside of the body cavity, cutting the organs loose by feeling for the connective tissue. The hardest part of this is disconnecting the colon without making a mess.

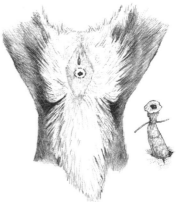

Make an incision around the anus, under the tail, and tie the bung shut.

DISCONNECT THE COLON. Return to the area where you cut around the anus and genitals and cut deeply with your knife in a circle all around that area. The goal will be to pull out the urethra and the colon, intact, through the pelvis. You'll want to avoid getting feces on the meat. If the bladder is full, it will be readily apparent to you. For obvious reasons, do not cut open the bladder.

Alternatively, instead of pushing the colon out through the center of the pelvis, it is possible to crack open the pelvis. In a young deer, you can often use a knife to cut through the part of the pelvis that faces you. The pelvis of an older deer will be more difficult to crack without using a hatchet.

Having disconnected the anus, genitals, and colon from the back end while keeping them attached to the rest of the guts, it is time to start getting all the internal organs out of the deer. Roll the deer over partway if working with the deer on the ground, and the guts will come about halfway out of the cavity (the attachment to the organs in the upper chest will prevent them from spilling out completely). With the intestines and rumen partially out, you will have better access to the diaphragm.

CUTTING THE DIAPHRAGM. The diaphragm is a membrane of flesh that separates the upper chest cavity (containing the heart and lungs) from the digestive system. It is easy to cut through.

Cutting through the diaphragm should give you a good view of the upper cavity. Get ready for things to get messy. You're going to have to

What to Bring on the Hunt

IF YOU'RE ACTUALLY HUNTING in your own backyard, there isn't much you'll need to pack. Your rifle, ammo, hunting license, and blaze orange will do just fine; you can always go back to the house for anything else. But for those who plan on hunting in a more remote area, here is a list of basics that would be smart to bring along.

○ Rifle
○ Ammunition
○ Hunting license
○ Blaze-orange clothing sufficient to meet local regulations
○ First-aid kit
○ Topographical map (in a ziplock bag to protect it from moisture)
○ Compass
○ Hunting knife
○ Backup knife
○ Sharpening stone
○ 10-foot length of rope
○ Cell phone
○ Water

○ Emergency space blanket
○ Lighter and matches
○ Snacks that can be eaten silently (avoid crinkly wrappers, or repackage such snacks into plastic baggies in advance)
○ Signaling mirror (any small mirror; even an old compact will do)
○ Emergency whistle
○ Water purification tablets
○ Toilet paper or tissues (aside from the obvious use, this highly visible yet biodegradable material makes a good "trail of bread crumbs")

Optional
○ Monopod, bipod, or shooting sticks
○ Grunt tube
○ Estrous bleat call
○ Hand warmers
○ Hatchet
○ Folding chair or stool

reach into that upper chest cavity and start cutting away the blood vessels and connective tissue that hold the heart, lungs, and liver in place. It's easiest to do one side first, then turn over the deer's body to repeat the process on the other side. The last thing you'll do is cut the trachea as high up as you can easily reach.

At this point, the viscera should be completely severed from the cavity. Tip over the body of the deer to get out the organs. There will also be quite a bit of blood pouring out from the chest cavity.

You're done with the field dressing now, and the worst is over. Quartering, skinning, and butchering are all far less repulsive activities than is gutting.

BRINGING IT HOME

After you've gutted the deer, you'll need to get it home. It helps to have two people for this job, but you can do it by yourself if you need to.

When hunting deer, always carry a short length of rope (about 10 feet long should suffice) in case you need to move a whole deer. If you intend to move the whole deer to another location after gutting it, tie one end of this rope around the back legs just above the joints. Tied tight at this point, the rope will not slip off. Make a handle for the other end of the rope, so that you can drag the deer without having the rope cut into your hands. For this task, I've used everything from my collapsed monopod to sticks picked up in the woods.

Some people use contraptions like game carts or ATVs with trailers to transport a dead deer out of the field. These work fine, though I myself don't care to spend the money on any of that when all I really need is a piece of rope and a stick. (Besides, the exercise is probably good for me.)

The one thing that really doesn't work well for transporting a dead deer is tying its legs together over a long pole and carrying it out with a partner, each of you with an end of the pole on your shoulder. It looks reasonable enough in cartoons, but unless you're both very tall, the deer's head will drag along the ground. The method might work better if the head could be secured upward somehow. Fashioning a sort of stretcher along two poles, with the deer lying on top of it, would work better.

Wilderness Survival

IT'S EASY TO GET used to accepting the risk of injuries in civilized situations. After all, a twisted ankle on a soccer field is little more than an inconvenience. Someone will be there to help you to the car or call an ambulance if necessary.

Everything is different when you're hunting in real wilderness. You might not always have a cell phone signal.

Twisting your ankle on a rocky hillside an hour before dark in the middle of winter is a mistake that could cost you your life. The most common causes of death in the outdoors are falling, drowning, and hypothermia. To avoid these, never run down a hill and don't climb over rocks or boulders that you don't need to. Be slow and cautious when moving over any sort of difficult terrain. Stay away from steep slopes, don't try to cross frozen water, and avoid other risks that could lead to injuries that expose you to hypothermia.

Every time you go out into a wilderness area to hunt or hike, be prepared to survive a night out in the worst conditions that could possibly be thrown at you. Wear clothes that will keep you warm and dry. Bring multiple methods of starting a fire, and make sure you know how to do so. Carry one or more emergency space blankets, which weigh only about an ounce each but can save your life by reflecting your body's heat back to you. Carry some food and water. Bring a whistle to blow so that people can find you. Learn how to make a simple lean-to in the woods to stay out of a blizzard or heavy rain. Always tell someone trustworthy exactly where you are hunting and when you expect to return. If you find that you're lost, stop moving; otherwise, you're likely only to get farther away from where people will come looking for you. Stay warm, stay dry, and stay calm.

Quartering in the Field

It is less conventional to quarter the deer (removing the upper portions of all four legs) in the field, rather than bringing home the entire deer, but I believe it's the ideal method for people who are hunting for food. This way you can completely strip the carcass of meat, leaving most of the skeleton, the head, and other remnants to return to the ground from which they grew, and not have to carry the extra weight and awkward volume of an entire deer. All the meat will fit in a large cooler in your car's trunk, making a pickup truck unnecessary.

Quartering a deer and stripping it of all the edible meat out there in the woods or field is not especially difficult or time-consuming, and I have done it in as little as half an hour. You'll be doing the final butchering — cutting the quarters into discrete cuts, steaks, roasts — in the comfort of your own kitchen.

If you do choose to quarter your deer in the field, be sure to carry several plastic bags with your cooler. One of them can be filled with the smaller scraps of rib meat and neck meat and such. I like to grind much of this meat, holding back some amount for making jerky and perhaps stew. The other bag is designated for less-pleasant-looking scraps our dogs and cats enjoy (see page 140).

NO GUTTING NECESSARY. Here's a secret about quartering in the field that is worth knowing: If you're quartering right away, you don't even need to gut the deer. Forgoing gutting altogether means you'll miss out on the tenderloins, since those are accessible only by gutting. In a small deer, however, those tenderloins might not amount to much anyway. Alternatively, you could remove just the digestive system to reach the tenderloins and leave the diaphragm and cardiovascular system intact.

Consider the path of the bullet through your deer before making the decision as to whether to gut or go straight to the quartering. Gut-shot deer are very unpleasant to dissect. You may also want to base your decision about gutting on the ambient temperature. Early in the season, you may have an unusually hot day and find that at 70°F (21°C) or higher the meat is at risk of rapid spoilage. In that situation, I absolutely believe it is best to quarter first and get the majority of the meat into the cooler before going in for the offal and tenderloins — if the abdomen hasn't started to bloat.

COURTESY

Before leaving the area where you gutted or quartered the deer, please consider the chance that someone will stumble across this particular scene within the next few days. Scavengers will usually devour the entire gut pile within 48 hours, often in much less time than that; I have seen a gut pile disappear almost completely within 8 hours.

But if you are within sight of a path used by nonhunters, it would be polite to bury the gut pile. You should also bury the gut pile if you're hunting on someone else's land where they allow their dogs to run freely on the property. The odds of being invited back for the next season drop considerably if the lady of the house is presented with a severed large intestine by her Labrador retriever.

Snout-to-Tail

I'M ENTIRELY IN FAVOR of snout-to-tail eating . . . as long as it's someone else doing it. I've never much cared for the taste of liver or kidneys, though I do often use these organs in making dog food. My dogs need to eat, too, and the food has to come from somewhere.

If you practice snout-to-tail eating, bear in mind that a deer killed by a hunting bullet is, by definition, going to have some of its internal organs blasted quite to pieces. You may find that a shot that has raked through the heart and lungs and on through the digestive system has rendered many of those organs essentially inedible.

If it is important to you that the organs be intact, you may want to master the brain shot and limit yourself to whatever range you find necessary to hit that small and moving target.

CHAPTER NINE

BUTCHERING

Some people choose to take their gutted deer to a butcher to turn the carcass into individual cuts of meat. This avoids a lot of work, of course. But it's an additional expense and may result in lower yield and lower-quality meat, depending on who processes the deer (see Deer Processors, page 147). Because of this, it's a good idea to learn to butcher your own deer. The job isn't as difficult as you might think and doesn't require many tools.

Quartering

The first step in butchering a gutted deer is quartering. *Quartering* is the process of removing the upper portions of all four legs, each of which is often referred to as a *quarter*. The only tool you really need for this job is a very sharp knife. You can use the same knife you used for gutting, but be sure to clean it and sharpen the blade before starting to quarter. It will have become blunted enough during the gutting process to require a new edge.

SHARPENING YOUR KNIFE

A blunt knife is more dangerous than a sharp knife. With a razor-sharp knife, you'll find that very little force is required to make a cut. As long as you keep the fingers of your other hand out of the way, you're unlikely to hurt yourself. A blunt knife requires more force to cut, and it is this application of force that most often leads to a knife's slipping and causing serious injury. To avoid this, remember to keep your knife sharp. I sharpen my knife after gutting, as well as halfway through the quartering process. Sharpening takes only a few minutes, and it is worth the trouble. A $5 knife with a razor-sharp blade is a better tool than a $200 knife with a dull edge.

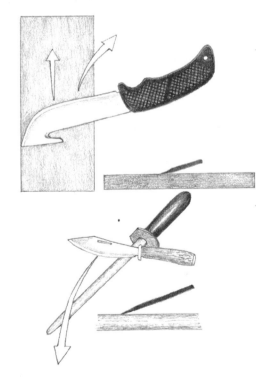

Using both a sharpening stone and a butcher's steel will help you to keep a good edge on your knife.

LAYING IT OR HANGING IT

I prefer to lay the deer on its side, on a section of clean pavement or stone, to butcher it. Other people hang their deer from a tree branch or a rafter. If you use that method, be sure to anchor the bottom of the deer to the ground or it will spin and sway awkwardly as you try to work on it. A large, counter-height outdoor table would work well, too; just make sure it's one you don't mind getting some blood on.

COVERING THE TARSAL GLANDS

Before starting, find the *tarsal glands* on the rear legs of the deer and cover them (I usually use duct tape). The tarsal glands produce a strong scent that deer use to communicate. If you touch a tarsal gland and then touch the meat, you'll seriously affect the flavor. Details like this are commonly overlooked and are what give venison a reputation for tasting gamy. If processed correctly, it should taste more like very lean beef.

SKINNING THE DEER

The simplest way to skin a deer is to make a few incisions in the right places (see the illustration at right) and pull off the hide by hand. Make one incision around the neck, just below the head, and one around the middle joint of each leg. Then start pulling down the hide by hand. After those initial incisions, the less you use a knife for skinning, the better. Skinning with a knife tends to result in rather a lot of meat stuck to the hide. Not only would that make more work if you decide to have the hide tanned, but it also compromises the condition of the meat.

Tarsal glands

Make your incisions along the dotted lines before you start skinning the deer.

Pulling off the hide instead of cutting it leaves a thin membrane over the muscle tissue that helps protect the meat from contamination.

If the deer is on the ground and you need to keep leaf litter off the meat, you should skin and butcher the entire side of the deer that is facing upward. This way the meat on the bottom side is protected by the hide while you skin and butcher the top side. When that top side has been completely stripped of meat, flip it over to work on the other side. If you have the deer suspended from a rope rather than on the ground, you should skin the whole deer at once, working from top to bottom.

Keep in mind that the neck contains a surprising amount of meat and should not be neglected in the skinning and butchering process. The lower legs, however, do not contain any edible meat — just tendons and connective tissue that are controlled by muscles in the upper legs — so don't bother skinning the lower legs unless you're curious to understand the anatomy or have a use for the cannon bone.

Along the initial incision you made when gutting the deer there are probably a pair of flaps of fairly tattered and dirty-looking tissue. Cut those off and discard them.

REMOVING THE FOREQUARTERS

Start by removing a forequarter. Pull it upward toward the head, and look at the underside to get a good idea of where one muscle group stops and another begins. Start carefully cutting that forequarter free from the bottom (the deer's armpit, essentially). You will notice that the connection of the forequarter to the torso of the deer is surprisingly weak. There is no socket, and the bones are floating against each other rather than being firmly connected. Cut a little muscle, and the forequarter will lift away easily.

CUT OFF THE LOWER LEG. Remove the lower leg from the excised forequarter. There are three ways to do this. You could work with the tip of your knife to cut each of the individual bands of connective tissue and tendon that hold the joint together. This takes practice to do quickly, but once you become familiar with those tendons, it will be the easiest way. You could saw off the lower leg, if such a tool is handy. Often I will strike a quick single blow with an ax to remove the lower leg, mostly because I happen to have a woodpile and an ax right near the spot where I usually quarter my deer.

If it is warmer outside than it is in your refrigerator, bring each quarter of meat into the kitchen as soon as it is free of hide and lower leg. Most refrigerators can easily fit an entire deer's worth of quarters in the lower drawers.

REMOVING THE BACKSTRAPS

Having dealt with the forequarters, it's time to remove the backstraps, my favorite cut of venison. Every deer has two backstraps, one along each side of the spine, running from the edge of the hindquarter to the base of the neck. It is a very fine thing to remove each backstrap in one long, continuous piece, which may then be coiled up neatly. The cut is analogous to a pork loin. Once the forequarter is no longer covering the front of the backstrap, you can get it all the way off to the hind quarter with only two long cuts. I consider the job of removing the backstraps to be the best test of a deer butcher's skills.

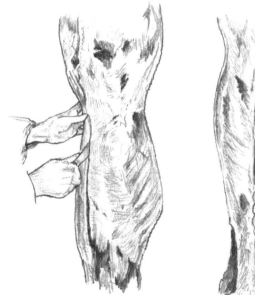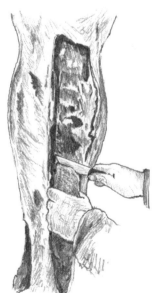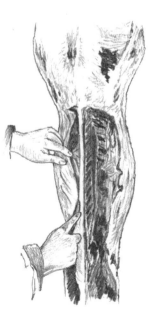

Always cut close to the bone when removing the backstraps.

Consider the geometry of the vertebrae and how they meet with the ribs. Slip your knife in along the center of the spine and work all the way down from one end to the other. Work as close to the bone as you possibly can. Take care to slice as smoothly as possible rather than using a sawing motion. One long cut is far better than many smaller cuts.

When you run into the top of the hindquarter, terminate the backstrap at that point. Package the backstrap in a large ziplock bag and put it in the refrigerator.

REMOVING THE HINDQUARTERS

The hindquarters are a bit more work than the forequarters. You will have to work from both the outside and the inside of the leg in order to get each hindquarter off neatly.

Like the forequarter, start from the inside. Work close to the bone to separate the muscle from the pelvis. Flex the joint, and feel where the ball and socket are. Use the tip of your knife to cut away the bands of tissue that hold the two bones of the joint together. Soon the ball will slip right out of the socket. Then there will be more muscle and connective tissue that is fairly self-explanatory. If you chose to crack the pelvis rather than ream it during the gutting stage, you can often lift the hindquarter right out with that side of the pelvis still attached.

Remove the lower legs from the hindquarters in the same fashion as you did those of the forequarters.

Depending on exactly how you separated the backstrap from a hindquarter, you may find that there is a big hunk of meat remaining just above where the hindquarter was. Remove this chunk of meat and package and label it separately, because it is a very tender and flavorful cut.

REMOVING THE TENDERLOIN

There is one more really nice cut of meat remaining. That is the tenderloin. Look inside the rib cage to the underside of the spine, just a bit forward of where the hindquarters were. You will see a smallish bit of muscle there; this is the most tender piece of meat in the entire deer. Do your best to cut it out carefully and in one piece, working close to the bone.

SAVING LESS DESIRABLE PIECES

Everything left is muscle to use for stew meat or to run through the grinder — neck and rib meat and anything else you see remaining. I bring out two big bowls or bags for this part. Into one I put everything that I'll be using for stew and grinding. Into the other I place all the undesirable bits of flesh, including hunks of fat (most deer fat tastes bad, has a grainy texture, and has a much higher melting point than beef or pork fat), tissue from around the bullet hole, and any other piece of meat that isn't large enough to merit trimming or cleaning. The contents of this latter bowl will be cooked up into dog food, so that nothing is wasted.

Neck meat tends to be pretty tough unless it is from a very young deer. Usually, it is most practical to grind it or use it for stews, where it will be slow-cooked for improved texture. Neck meat from a very large deer could be cut into a few roasts, but some extra effort to tenderize it would be required.

When you can see through the rib cage, you know you've done a thorough job of stripping the carcass.

Deer Processors

SOME OF THE BUSINESSES that process deer for hunters during the season do a very good job. Many do not. In fact, it's not even guaranteed that you'll get back meat from the same deer that you dropped off. Even though you've been prompt in gutting and cooling down your deer and scrupulous in keeping any matter from within the digestive system from spilling out and tainting the flavor of the meat, you can't be sure that some other hunter has done the same.

Also, a professional deer processor may not care as much about getting off every little scrap of meat. He's got 20 other deer lined up behind yours. Removing *most* of the meat might be good enough for his standards. Is that good enough for your standards?

Processing the Meat

Having finished this process of quartering and initial processing, you now have four quarters and a pile of sundry other meat. I recommend dry-aging the hindquarters and finishing the packaging of the other meat right away (or perhaps you can save that processing until tomorrow if it's been a very long, hard day of hunting and dressing).

DRY-AGING THE HINDQUARTERS

Dry-aging is the process of letting meat sit or hang unwrapped at a cool temperature for a period of 5 to 7 days. Dry-aging your meat will do two very nice things to it. First, the meat becomes more tender. Meat contains natural enzymes that will break down the collagen fibers contained within the muscle. As an animal gets older, the amount of cellulose in its body increases, and as a result its meat becomes tough. In an older deer especially, the texture of the meat improves dramatically after 5 to 7 days of aging. The second advantage of dry-aging is that moisture gradually evaporates from the meat, concentrating flavor in the remaining volume of tissue.

Let it be perfectly clear that the aging process is not *controlled rot*, as some people seem to believe. Rotting is the process of bacteria digesting the meat and leaving behind their bad-tasting and potentially dangerous waste products. Dry-aging meat is simply allowing the natural enzymes of the meat to break down the collagen while some evaporation is occurring. No bacteria required.

IN THE REFRIGERATOR. Commercially dry-aged beef is usually stored unwrapped in a special refrigerated facility until it is ready. You can achieve similar results by aging venison in your refrigerator. Clear out the crisper and meat drawers and store the quarters inside. Turn down the temperature of the fridge as low as you can without causing your milk to freeze. Each day, be sure to turn and rotate the quarters so that all sides get even airflow and the whole surface dries out. Admittedly, the surface of the meat will not look very appetizing at this point. That's okay because you're going to carve away the rind after the meat has finished aging.

AGING FOR 5 TO 7 DAYS. Allow the meat to age for no less than 5 days but ideally no more than 7. Because of the limited amount of airflow in a refrigerator, after 7 days mold and rot will begin to set in. Less than 5 days isn't enough time for the enzymes to break down the muscle fibers. Note that if the meat is allowed to freeze, the enzymes will work at a tiny fraction of the pace they would at above-freezing temperatures.

BUTCHERING THE AGED HINDQUARTERS

When your meat has finished aging, it's time to do the final butchering. You're going to carve off the hard rind that formed on the outside of the quarters and turn the remaining meat into roasts, steaks, cutlets, and ground meat. Start by gathering some basic materials.

REQUIRED

- A very sharp knife, not too long (maybe even the same one you used for gutting and quartering)
- Some type of large cutting board
- Ziplock bags, shrink-wrap, or butcher's paper in which to wrap cuts of meat

OPTIONAL

- A butcher's cleaver (in addition to the shorter knife)
- Butcher's block
- Meat grinder

CUTTING BOARD. A cutting board doesn't have to be anything fancy. I like to use a freestanding butcher's block, but any piece of scrap board would work just as well, as long as it's clean and has no dangerous chemicals in it (don't use plywood or any kind of pressure-treated wood).

It's important to sterilize your surface before putting food on it. You can prepare a mild bleach solution for this purpose by mixing a tablespoon of bleach with half a gallon of water. Bleach is a highly effective antibiotic agent in surprisingly low concentrations. Prepare this bleach solution in a bowl, and use paper towels or a sponge to swab down the cutting surface before starting. Both wood and well-used plastic are notorious for harboring bacteria, and you'll want to kill as much of those bacteria as possible.

Avoid Wood Treated with Boiled Linseed Oil

If you have a butcher's block in your home already, it may or may not be suitable for food preparation. A butcher's block, freestanding or built into a table or counter, must be oiled periodically to prevent it from drying out and cracking. The preferred oil for this job is linseed oil. But there are two types of linseed oil — regular and boiled. Boiled linseed oil is not only boiled; it also has metallic drying agents added to it. These help the oil dry out sooner and speed up the finishing of a piece of wood, but they are also poisonous to human beings.

Do not use boiled linseed oil on a food-preparation surface or on any surface that might be used by someone else to prepare food in the future. If you acquired a butcher's block secondhand and it was used as a piece of furniture rather than a surface for cutting meat, you would do well to assume that the previous owner used the wrong oil.

MEAT GRINDER. A meat grinder is a very handy thing to have when processing venison, and it will increase the efficiency with which you utilize the meat. Any odd little scrap of meat that is not big enough to make a cut of its own can be run through the grinder, and you will have many such pieces. There are professional-quality meat grinders that cost hundreds of dollars, but an inexpensive one will generally work just as well, as will a hand-cranked model. I have been very happy with the meat-grinding attachment for my KitchenAid mixer, which is relatively inexpensive.

PACKAGING. You need to pay more attention to the packaging of the meat if you expect to be storing it for a long time. If you think your household will go through the whole deer in the space of a few weeks, you can get away with wrapping meat neatly in butcher's paper, taping it shut, and sticking it in the freezer. If left in the freezer for more than a few weeks, however, meat will become freezer-burned when wrapped this way.

For longer storage, it's important to keep oxygen away from the meat. There are professional shrink-wrappers that can vacuum-wrap your meat, but the inexpensive versions for home use tend to be unreliable. Ziplock bags work a little better if you squeeze the air out carefully. The best bang for your packaging buck is the inexpensive ziplock bags that come with a sort of nipple to which a hand- or battery-powered pump is applied to suck out all the air. The pumps for these systems are very inexpensive, but they work well. I can recommend either the Reynolds Handi-Vac or the now-discontinued Ziploc Pump-n-Seal.

REMOVING THE RIND

Place your first hindquarter on the cutting board and start carving off the rind with your freshly sharpened knife. As you cut, you'll notice a few stratified layers in the meat: a hard, dark exterior layer (*the rind*), followed by a thin gray layer no more than a millimeter thick and under that a rich red layer. Your goal is to carve just under anything gray. The red interior is free of all bacteria and off flavors, and that is what you want. Don't cut any deeper than you have to, so as not to waste any of the good stuff.

This will take you a good long while the first time you do it, but will go faster as you get better at it. At first it might take you as long as half an hour to do a single hindquarter, but with skill it can be done in as little as 5 minutes. Don't rush it the first time, or you're likely to end up slicing yourself with the knife.

After carving off the rind, clean the cutting board and sterilize it again with the bleach solution. If there are any bacteria that have gotten a foothold in the rind, you don't want to introduce them into the nice, sound meat that is about to be packaged.

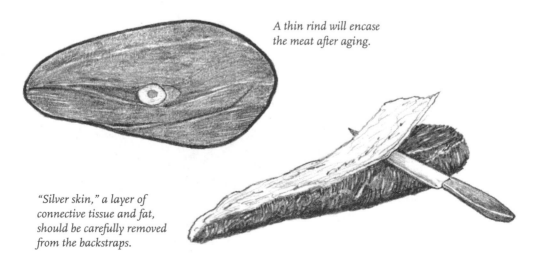

A thin rind will encase the meat after aging.

"Silver skin," a layer of connective tissue and fat, should be carefully removed from the backstraps.

BONING THE HINDQUARTER

The rindless quarter can now be cut into whatever individual serving sizes you prefer. Do get all the meat off the bones, then discard the bones (dogs love them). Carve out or peel off any fat you encounter (deer fat does not become marbled into the meat, the way beef fat does, and it tastes pretty bad).

When boning the meat off the hindquarters, start by finding the round end of the bone on the larger side of the quarter, and cut along that bone all the way until you come to the joint. Keep the knife very close to the bone. Then make a similar cut that skirts the shank and comes in to meet the end of your first cut at an angle. (Keep shank meat out of your hindquarter steaks, because it is very tough and full of connective tissue.)

You will then have a large piece of meat free from a hindquarter. If you've noticed a lot of fat on the deer overall, you should open up this piece of meat to find and remove the triangular pocket of fat that will be lurking within. To do this, cut along the seam on the newly cut side, butterfly the meat on that seam, and remove the bit of fat inside. On a deer with very little fat (which is common toward the end of the rut), this step is unnecessary.

This cut can be used as one great big roast, but I prefer to turn it into steaks and medallions. Separate out the butterflied sides, then slice them against the grain. Keep the cuts thicker than you would cut beef, since you don't want them to dry out quickly while cooking (I like them to be at least an inch thick). Remember to cut for consistent thickness in each piece, to avoid having one side cooked well-done while the other is rare. The oddly shaped little end pieces can go into the grinder, or use them for stir-fry.

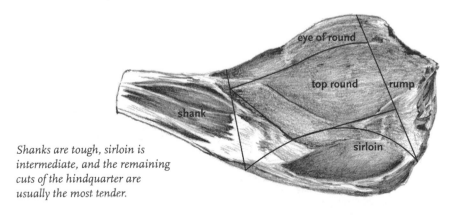

Shanks are tough, sirloin is intermediate, and the remaining cuts of the hindquarter are usually the most tender.

The procedure is much the same for the large piece of meat that composes the other side of the hindquarter, except that you will want to work the knife carefully around the bone to free the meat without waste. Always cut your steaks, roasts, and medallions against the grain.

COLLECTING SCRAPS

Keep a bowl handy for scraps to grind; it will fill up pretty quickly. Ground venison is good to have on hand because it can so easily be substituted for ground beef in standard recipes. You can usually use it as a straight substitution, except in recipes that require the meat to stick together well. Meatballs and burger patties can be made from venison, but you'll need to add some fat to keep it all together.

All the rind and fat and other discarded pieces you'll end up with don't have to be wasted if you have a dog. Put it all in the biggest casserole dish you have, then stick it in the oven at 350°F until it's all cooked through. I usually mix up these cooked scraps with a pot of rice to make wet dog food.

PROCESSING THE FOREQUARTERS

Forequarters are often too small to bother trying to age. Once a rind forms and is removed, there will be very little meat left. On a large deer, you might be able to get some steaks out of the forequarters, but on a typical doe, the forequarter meat is best used in smaller pieces. Run it through the grinder, cut it into slices for jerky, or use it for stew meat or a stir-fry. The whole forequarter can also be slow-cooked as one intact joint on the bone.

As long as you are starting out with well-butchered meat that has not been allowed to sit out in warm temperatures after being killed, you will find that cooking with venison is not very difficult. In most cases, you can use venison as a straight substitute for beef in recipes that call for it.

Wild venison contains very favorable ratios of omega-6 to omega-3 fatty acids (roughly 2 to 1). It is higher in cholesterol than beef, although it remains unclear how much of that is "good" versus "bad" cholesterol. Venison is high in protein, and like all other wild meat, it is not laced with any antibiotics or artificial growth hormones.

CHAPTER TEN

COOKING

Venison, properly butchered, tastes very much like lean beef. Also like beef, the texture varies based on the age of the animal and what part of the anatomy a particular cut was taken from. Compared to beef there is typically much less fat in venison. On the one hand, this offers health benefits to people on certain diets; on the other hand, it requires that special attention be paid to keep the meat moist while it's cooking.

The Myth of "Gaminess"

There is a pervasive myth that venison has a "gamy" taste that somehow needs to be disguised. Weigh the value of this reputation in light of the manner in which venison has historically been handled. The traditions surrounding the processing of venison in Western culture date to before artificial refrigeration was available and before hunters had any knowledge of the existence of bacteria or the chemistry of enzymes.

Many scions of old hunting families will tell you that a deer *must* be allowed to "hang" outdoors for at least a week before you begin to butcher it. If one could dictate the weather during that time, I suppose this might work. But if the carcass freezes, the aging process comes more or less to a halt. And if the temperature creeps up into the mid-40s or higher, the meat will begin to spoil. These same "traditional" hunters will also stress the importance of using lots of juniper berry or other seasonings to mask the gamy flavor of the meat. The direct relationship between these two practices somehow fails to sink in.

If you treated beef, pork, lamb, or chicken in the same way that venison is so often treated, all those meats would taste gamy. Gaminess is not a feature of a particular type of meat but rather the result of poor butchering practices. It's a vague term that usually describes some combination of bacterial contamination and scent from the tarsal glands.

Consider the broad variety of creatures said to have a gamy flavor: deer, squirrels, ducks, pheasants, rabbits, bears, and so on. These animals hold very different positions on the evolutionary tree and subsist on different diets. It seems suspicious to me that they should all be said to have a similar flavor. In truth, these meats have only one relevant thing in common: they are frequently dressed and butchered by amateurs who learned their methods through an oral tradition dating back to before anyone had heard of *E. coli*.

Slow, sloppy handling of meat tends to lead to a gamy flavor. It doesn't need to be that way. Simply keep dirt and hair off the meat and get it packaged and refrigerated as quickly as possible under sanitary conditions. Then it won't taste gamy.

Making Substitutions

Venison is very low in fat. This is seen as an advantage by most people these days, but it also means that it must be cooked differently from the way you would beef. When cooking venison, you've got to make an extra effort to keep the meat moist. If you try to cook up a piece of venison the same way you'd cook a T-bone steak, for example (usually by searing it and putting it, uncovered, in the oven or under the broiler), you'll be disappointed. Some cuts are similar, though; the texture, flavor, and fat content of venison from the hindquarters and backstraps are reminiscent of those in a fine-grained filet mignon.

There are a great many recipes calling for beef that can be followed faithfully, the only change being the substitution of venison. Almost any recipe calling for ground beef — chili, pasta sauce, tacos, for example — can be made with venison in exactly the same way you would with beef. The exception is recipes for meatballs and hamburgers. (The lack of fat marbled into the meat means that burger patties and meatballs will not hold together very well on their own without some form of fat added, or by combining venison with beef. Fifteen to 20 percent beef added to the grinder is usually sufficient; you can use pork or lamb for the same purpose. One egg ground with a pound of venison works nicely as well. And some people use mushrooms to good effect as an adhesion agent.)

Rather than adding beef, I prefer to grind and package most of my scraps as straight venison, but I'll also grind 3 or 4 pounds out of each deer blended with beef to have on hand for burgers. Be sure to label each package of ground meat as to what it has been mixed with, if anything. Also write the date on the bags, so you can be sure to use up the first deer of the season before moving on to the next one.

In addition to grinding scraps, you can grind up meat from the shanks. Alternatively, use them for any kind of slow cooking; they're excellent in the sort of stew that simmers in a slow cooker all day long.

Venison Stroganoff

Stroganoff is easy to prepare, and this recipe cooks up very quickly.

SERVES FOUR

4 cups hot beef or venison broth	½ cup merlot
Butter	⅓ cup ketchup
1½ pounds cubed venison	¼ cup flour
4 cups sliced mushrooms	Paprika
1 large onion, thinly sliced	Salt and pepper
2 large cloves garlic, minced	1 cup sour cream

Heat the beef or venison broth to just under a simmer. Brown the venison, mushrooms, onion, and garlic in butter in a large skillet. Add the wine and pour half of the broth into the skillet. Bring the mixture to a simmer for 5 minutes. Add the ketchup and stir it in well.

Whisk the flour into the remaining hot beef broth until it reaches the consistency of a thin batter. Stir the flour-broth mixture into the skillet until the sauce begins to thicken. Add salt, pepper, and paprika to taste. Remove from the heat and stir in the sour cream. Serve over egg noodles or rice.

Venison Jerky

Consider this jerky marinade to be merely a starting point. When making jerky, I rarely stick to a particular recipe. It's much more fun to poke around in the spice cabinet and to look for interesting sauces in the fridge that could be combined for something new: a spicy Thai pepper paste, a barbecue sauce, even salad dressing. There are probably all sorts of half-filled and forgotten bottles in the back of your refrigerator that could be the basis for a batch of deer jerky.

2 pounds venison
1 cup teriyaki sauce
3 tablespoons soy sauce
2 teaspoons lemon juice
1 teaspoon celery salt

½ teaspoon paprika
Quite a lot of freshly ground
   black pepper

Slice the venison into thin strips that are no more than ¼ inch thick. Remove any connective tissue and fat. Mix the teriyaki sauce, soy sauce, lemon juice, celery salt, and paprika in a bowl or a gallon-size ziplock bag. Add the sliced venison strips. Be sure to coat all surfaces of every strip. If you are using a ziplock bag, seal the top and shake it well. Put the meat in the refrigerator to marinate for 1 hour.

Preheat the oven to 170°F. Spread the soaked strips of venison in a single layer on a metal cooling rack of the type used for cookies and cakes. Grind as much pepper over the meat as you think you'll be able to stand. Place the rack in the oven; put a rimmed cookie sheet underneath the rack of meat to catch the marinade as it drips off.

Heat for 2 hours, then remove the rack from the oven and turn over every piece of jerky. Grind more pepper onto this side. Return the rack to the oven for at least another 2 hours. If you prefer moist, chewy jerky, remove the meat after a total of 4 hours of drying. For bone-dry jerky, let it go for a total of 6 hours.

Almost-Butterflied Venison Parmesan

The basic technique of carving out a little pocket inside the meat presents all sorts of possibilities. I have enjoyed using blue cheese in place of Parmesan, but you can stuff the pocket with whatever catches your fancy.

SERVES TWO

2 venison hindquarter steaks at least 1 inch thick	Several sprigs of fresh rosemary
¼ cup sliced Parmesan cheese	

Preheat the oven to 350°F. Using a paring knife (to be perfectly honest, I do most of my food prep with my hunting knives), slice a pocket along the inside of each steak. This is like butterflying the meat, only you don't go all the way through: the meat ends up with a pocket like that of a piece of pita bread.

Stuff each pocket with half the Parmesan and half the rosemary. (It's better to use slices than grated cheese, as it's difficult to prevent grated cheese from running out the side of a pocket.) Put the steaks in a casserole and cook, covered, just to medium-rare (the internal temperature should register 135–140°F on a meat thermometer). Pan-searing the steaks in butter for some color before putting them in the oven is a worthy variation.

Serve with a cold pale ale or a pinot grigio.

Thyme and Butter Coiled Backstrap

This always looks magnificent on a serving dish. You can substitute tarragon for the thyme, if you'd like.

SERVES FOUR TO SIX

One venison backstrap

1 tablespoon Worcestershire sauce

A handful of fresh thyme

¼ cup butter

Pinot noir, for deglazing and as an accompaniment

Trim the backstrap. One side will be covered with a thick "silver skin" similar to that found on many cuts of lamb. The best practice is to remove the entire thing in one smooth cut, losing as little meat as possible in the process.

A good technique is to lay the backstrap flat with the silver skin facing down near the edge of a counter or butcher block. Using a very sharp cleaver, start the cut at the closer end of the backstrap, holding the cleaver parallel to the counter. Slide the backstrap slowly and firmly back against the stable cleaver, shaving off the unwanted material. Remove any other exposed connective tissues on all sides of the backstrap, but be careful not to chase them too deeply into the meat or you'll find that you've taken apart the entire thing.

Preheat the oven to 350°F, and heat a skillet to use for searing. Drizzle the Worcestershire sauce along the length of the backstrap, then spread the butter and sprinkle the thyme over the meat.

Roll the backstrap into a tight coil. Either tie it together with a bit of string (an organic material only — nylon or plastic cord will melt in the oven) or use wooden kebab skewers to secure it. (Any old twig sharpened with a pocketknife will do the job just as well.)

Sear the coiled backstrap in the butter. When it's nicely brown, transfer the backstrap to a casserole dish. Deglaze the skillet with a bit of the pinot noir, then pour the juices over the meat. Set the casserole dish in the oven and cook, covered, until no more than rare — 130°F on a meat thermometer. The difference between rare and medium for most cuts of venison is the difference between a perfect piece of meat that can be cut with a spoon and a lump of gray shoe leather.

Serve with a bottle of the same pinot noir used to deglaze the pan.

Boboti

This traditional South African meat loaf is quite moist and therefore a bit looser than the run-of-the-mill variety. The seasonings turn an ordinary meal into something special.

SERVES FOUR

- 1 onion, chopped
- 1 clove of garlic, chopped
- 2 tablespoons butter or olive oil
- 1–2 tablespoons curry powder
- 1 teaspoon turmeric
- 1 pound ground venison
- 3–4 eggs (2 for the meat, 1 or 2 for the topping)
- ½ cup bread crumbs moistened in 4 tablespoons of milk
- ¼ cup raisins or sultanas (optional)
- 6 tablespoons chutney or apricot jam
- 4 bay leaves

Preheat the oven to 350°F. Brown the onion and the garlic in the oil; add the curry powder and turmeric. In a large bowl, mix the venison, 2 beaten eggs, the bread crumbs, the raisins, and the chutney. Add the onion and garlic and blend well. Mold the mixture into a greased loaf pan. Top with the remaining beaten egg(s) and the bay leaves. Bake, uncovered, for 1 hour, until cooked through.

Venison Chili

This chili recipe uses white beans rather than the traditional kidney or pinto beans. The corn provides a nice crunch and a pop of sweetness to offset the spiciness.

SERVES 8

1 pound ground venison
½ onion, chopped
⅛ cup chopped garlic
2 tablespoons olive oil
1 46-ounce can of diced tomatoes
1 15-ounce can of northern or navy beans
1 15-ounce can of corn (creamed corn can be used as well)
¼ cup chili powder

1 tablespoon salt (or to taste)
1 teaspoon paprika
1 tablespoon dried oregano
1 teaspoon dried sage (1½ tablespoons fresh)
½ teaspoon cayenne (more for extra heat)
1 teaspoon black pepper
4 cups cooked medium- or long-grain rice
   Grated cheese
   Sour cream
   Chopped cilantro

Brown the venison, onion, and garlic in the olive oil in a medium-size stock pot. Add the tomato, beans, corn, spices, and salt. Simmer at least 25 minutes, up to 1 hour (or slow-cook it), until the flavors are well blended. Serve over a bed of rice, or the rice can be added to the chili itself. Add the cheese, sour cream, and cilantro, to taste.

Sauerbraten

Our important family events usually include this traditional, slow-cooked German dish. It takes time, but the result is well worth the wait.

SERVES 8

5-pound venison roast

FOR THE MARINADE

- 1½ cups cider vinegar
- 2 cups apple juice
- ½ cup red wine
- 1 large onion, chopped
- 3 bay leaves
- 1 teaspoon powdered cloves (1 tablespoon whole cloves)
- 1 teaspoon cinnamon
- 1 teaspoon powdered ginger
- ½ teaspoon allspice
- ½ teaspoon nutmeg
- 1 teaspoon black pepper

FOR THE SAUERBRATEN

- 1 carrot, chopped
- 1 green pepper, chopped
- 1 onion, chopped
- ½ cup raisins or sultanas
- ¼ to ⅓ cup brown sugar (adjust to taste after cooking for a while)

To make the marinade, mix together all the marinade ingredients in a large bowl. Put in the meat, cover, and marinate in the refrigerator for 5 days.

Remove the venison and brown it over medium heat in a skillet. Transfer the meat to a slow cooker. Strain the marinade and add it to the slow cooker, enough to cover the venison, chopped vegetables, raisins, and sugar (save the extra marinade to add while cooking, if needed), and let cook for at least 6 hours.

When venison is very tender, remove it to a platter. Strain the cooking liquid, then thicken it with ground gingerbread or gingersnap cookies. Ladle it over the meat. Serve with stewed red cabbage and spaetzle. Heaven!

Bibimbap

This is an excellent way to use leftover venison and vegetables (including lettuce). The ingredients here are ones I often find in my own kitchen, but you can use anything you like, in any amounts. Keep vegetables separate when marinating and cooking; part of the joy of Bibimbap is getting to stir everything together with your spoon.

Leftover venison steak, sliced
   thin
Summer squash, julienned
Zucchini, julienned
Carrot, julienned
Apple or pear, chopped
Green onion, sliced
Fresh spinach
Eggs (1 egg for each serving)
Leftover rice
Chili sauce

MARINADE
3 tablespoons rice wine or
   apple juice
3 tablespoons dark soy sauce
1 tablespoon sesame oil
1 tablespoon minced garlic
1 teaspoon minced ginger
1 teaspoon sugar
  A few shakes of sesame
   seeds

SIMPLE CHILI SAUCE
½ cup applesauce
¼ cup sriracha chili sauce
1 tablespoon sesame seeds

Mix together chili sauce ingredients and set aside. Prepare the marinade. Individually coat the steak and the vegetables (except the spinach) with the marinade and let sit for about 15 minutes. Separately, give each vegetable and the steak a quick stir-fry. (Use a large pan if you want to cook everything together.) Fry 1 egg for each serving. Heat the rice.

Fill a large bowl two-thirds full with the rice. Arrange individual vegetables and the meat in sections over the rice, then top with a fried egg and a dollop of chili sauce.

Now take a long spoon and stir!

Serve with kimchee, if you're lucky enough to have some.

Venison and Sweet Potato Curry

The softness of the sweet potato is a great complement to venison. The peas add a nice texture to the curry.

SERVES SIX

- 2 tablespoons concentrated Thai red curry paste (or to taste)
- 14 ounces coconut milk
- 14 ounces beef stock
- 2 large sweet potatoes, cubed
- 1 pound stew meat
- 2–3 tablespoons olive oil or butter
- ½ onion, finely chopped
- 6 cloves garlic, chopped
  Splash of beer or white wine, for deglazing (optional)
- 1 cup green peas
- 2 tablespoons grated ginger
- 2 tablespoons turbinado sugar (or 2 tablespoons sugar with a dribble of molasses)
- ¼ cup fish sauce
- 2–3 tablespoons sesame oil
  Salt and pepper
  Chopped green onion

Thin the curry paste with a few tablespoons of water or some of the coconut milk or stock. Steam the sweet potatoes until partially cooked (firm but able to be pierced with a fork), and set aside. In a medium-size stock pot or Dutch oven over medium heat, sauté the onion in the olive oil, then brown the meat. Add the garlic during the last two minutes. Deglaze the pan, using the beer if you'd like, then add the stock, coconut milk, sweet potatoes, peas, ginger, sugar, fish sauce, sesame oil and curry paste. Add salt and pepper to taste, then simmer for at least 1 hour. (This recipe also works well in a slow cooker.)

Serve over a bed of long-grain rice and garnish with the green onion to taste.

CHAPTER ELEVEN

WHERE TO HUNT

Most of us are not fortunate enough to own a large tract of rural land on which to hunt. Fortunately, it's not really necessary to have access to a *lot* of land to hunt successfully. As long as there are deer in the general vicinity of a property and you can legally discharge a firearm or shoot a bow, it's very likely that you can bag a deer for food on that property.

In Your Own Backyard

You really might very well be able to hunt deer in, yes, your own back-yard. This is the ideal situation for food hunters: zero food miles. It doesn't require driving, and you don't have to carry the meat far to get it into the kitchen. And there's a special satisfaction in eating the same deer that's been eating the tomatoes and lettuce out of your garden for the past year.

I've been feeding my family the majority of our animal protein for several years mostly by hunting my own 6 acres. This piece of land is so tiny that most deer hunters wouldn't even consider taking it seriously as hunting land. But remember, I'm not pursuing trophy bucks. When you aren't too picky about whether you shoot a doe or a buck, deer hunting gets a lot easier.

BAITING

Many states and counties have laws against hunting deer over bait — that is, setting out food specifically to draw deer in so you can shoot them — so be sure to check the regulations that apply in your area. Even something as innocuous as a bird feeder may be considered a form of bait if you pull the trigger while deer are raiding it.

FOOD PLOTS. Usually, even in places where baiting is illegal, hunting over a food plot — an area specifically planted to appeal to deer — is legal. A food plot can be a very smart idea for a small backyard that has nothing else to attract deer during the hunting season. Remember that the hostas and other ornamentals that deer were eager to eat out of your garden during the spring may be in a less edible state by the time deer season rolls around. To bring deer in and hold them during the hunting season, you'll need to plant things that are ready to eat at that time.

Buckwheat, sorghum, and any kind of brassica (cabbage, broccoli, and the like) are all examples of good things to plant in a food plot for deer. There are many commercial seed mixtures you can buy and sow that are designed to ripen just in time for deer season. You don't need a lot of space for this. Even a patch of land as small as one-eighth of an acre can be a magnet for suburban deer.

When choosing a location for a food plot on a small parcel of land, keep in mind what your opportunities are for a safe shot. Try to choose a location where you will have a concealed place to shoot from, with a safe backstop behind the area where you're expecting the deer to appear. A tree stand might be a good idea in this situation, though a back deck may be able to serve the same purpose.

On Public Land

B eyond backyards, there are plenty of places to hunt deer in most states; a great deal of public land is available. Different types of public land have different primary and secondary purposes. If you intend to rely on public land to hunt on, it pays to understand the differences.

NATIONAL FORESTS

The National Forest Service was created in 1905 by President Theodore Roosevelt (as an expansion of a fledgling program started under President Benjamin Harrison in 1891). Its purpose was to set aside 100 million acres of mountainous timberland to be managed for long-term harvest. Long-term harvest of timber remains the primary purpose of national forests.

Most national forests also allow hunting and other forms of recreation, as long as they do not interfere with timber harvest. Your state and local hunting laws generally still apply to federal land within their boundaries. You'll have to pay a few dollars extra for a stamp on your hunting license that allows you to hunt in national forests, but it is well worth the small outlay. This money goes toward the worthy cause of maintaining the access roads and paying the salaries of forest rangers, and opens up millions of acres to you. Some national forests offer parking, access roads, and camping facilities.

Given the fact that neither recreation nor hunting is the primary use of the land, you should keep your expectations for the facilities low. Camping areas tend to be primitive, and sometimes the best hunting will be in areas where there are no trails or roads provided. Don't assume that it will be like a park with trash cans, signs, and shelters everywhere.

NATIONAL PARKS

National parks are often confused with national forests, but they are completely different. The primary purpose of a national park is to provide wild recreational opportunities for people. Despite the relative lack of use by hikers during the fall and winter months, all but one national park (Grand Teton National Park, in Wyoming) prohibit hunting by law. Often, a national park directly abuts a national forest, with the only access to the forest being to park your vehicle on the parkland and walk through it to reach the national forest. In these cases, be sure to look at the rules for transporting not only your rifle through the park but also a dead deer or a cooler full of meat back to your vehicle. It can all generally be done legally, but it is a good idea to let the park rangers know what you are doing ahead of time, to avoid any mistaken impressions that you are poaching within the boundaries of the park.

WILDLIFE REFUGES

The word *refuge* seems to imply that hunting wouldn't be encouraged at state and federal wildlife refuges, but in fact, hunting is not only welcome but also sometimes requested in these places. When deer populations get too large, especially in areas without natural predators, it can be beneficial to the other animals in the refuge for the deer to be thinned out. Often in those situations, the refuge will organize a managed hunt.

Managed hunts on refuges typically require preregistration, and the organizers will insist that you show up at a specific time and date. If you're willing to accommodate this, you may have the opportunity to hunt areas that are quite riddled with deer. Sometimes the catch is that access is limited the rest of the year and you might not be permitted to scout as much as you ought to.

NATIONAL PRESERVES AND RESERVES

National reserves and preserves are very similar to parks, except that they usually allow hunting (provided it does not interfere with the primary purpose of preserving whatever resource the land was set aside to protect). National preserves are federally managed, whereas national reserves (though still owned by the federal government) are managed by state and local authorities.

NATIONAL MONUMENTS

National monuments have become an odd category of public land in recent decades. The designation was once given only to very small parcels of what was already federal land that had some unusual or historic feature, such as Devil's Tower in northeastern Wyoming. Today, the designation has been used by presidents to protect wild areas of millions of acres. A president has the power to designate national monuments by executive order, which has served to protect many areas from logging and mining (while simultaneously confusing the basic intent of a monument). Although it's difficult to say what the primary purpose of some national monuments is, some of them are large enough to permit hunting.

NATIONAL WATERWAYS

A national seashore or lakeshore may sometimes allow hunting. If you have such a place near you, it's worth looking into the rules for that specific piece of land.

Hunting on State Land

STATE LAND USES VARY more than national land uses do. Many states have their own state forest system, which parallels the national program. Usually, hunting is allowed in state forests, but in some cases recreational use has increased over time and turned forestland into what is now effectively a park. In those situations, swimming areas, tennis courts, camping areas, and scenic drives spread throughout a forest might prompt the state to ban hunting in that particular state forest. A requirement that hunters purchase a separate state forest stamp on their license is becoming more and more common, as state game departments search for new sources of revenue.

In most state parks, though, rules are carefully set that place recreational areas of a park off-limits for hunting while the more wild areas are approved. This varies a great deal from one state and locality to another. If you have a state park close by, it's worth investigating as a potential hunting site.

MILITARY BASES

A military base, surprisingly enough, can be a great place to hunt. Many bases have large wilderness areas that are available to hunters — after getting approval. It would be a very bad idea to show up at a military base with a scoped rifle and wearing full camouflage if you do not have such approval. But this isn't usually hard to arrange, and many bases have a website to streamline the process. Your state game agency will probably have information and links to what you need.

WILDLIFE MANAGEMENT AREAS

Finally, we have that best kind of public land for our purposes: the wildlife management area. WMAs are the only category of public land with the primary purpose of providing a place for people to hunt and fish. From time to time, certain WMAs are temporarily off-limits for hunting while a threatened species is in recovery, but for the most part, this is land that's purchased by state game and wildlife agencies using money from hunting licenses, and it is maintained with the same source of revenue.

You're likely to hear older deer hunters downplay the idea of hunting on public land. Generally speaking, it has a reputation for being crowded with hunters and holding poor trophies. As a food hunter, though, you're not likely to care about trophies. And a lot of that land is not as crowded with hunters as some people might think. This reputation was cemented many decades ago, before hunting began to decline as an American pastime. Many of the old deer hunters who dismiss national forests and WMAs for hunting opportunities haven't ventured onto them since the late 1970s.

Even where there really are a lot of vehicles in the parking area on opening day, remember that most hunters (like most people) are basically lazy. Ninety percent of the hunters who arrived in those vehicles are probably sitting within a mile of the parking lot. If you're willing and able to hike farther, in a forest of millions of acres, it won't be difficult to get out to an area where you don't have any competition. Coming prepared to quarter in the field can also make you more competitive in this regard, as there are plenty of hunters who would be willing to hike to find deer but have learned the hard way about how difficult it is to carry a whole dead deer 2 or 3 miles back to the truck.

RESOURCES

WILDLIFE AGENCIES

Your state or provincial wildlife agency is an excellent resource for information about local hunting regulations and license requirements. Usually you can also find information about how to sign up for free hunting safety courses as well. All 50 American states (including Hawaii) and all 13 Canadian provinces have some type of deer that can be hunted, whether they're whitetails, blacktails, or mule deer. For a complete list of wildlife agencies, visit *www.fws.gov/offices/statelinks.html*.

FIREARM MAINTENANCE

For information about firearm maintenance and repair, I suggest looking at Midway USA's material on its YouTube channel (*www.youtube.com/user/MidwayUSA*). Midway is a retailer of gunsmithing supplies and it has created many excellent how-to videos demonstrating basic tasks involved with maintaining, disassembling, and setting up rifles and shotguns. When you take apart a gun and can't figure out how to put it back together, this is the place to go.

SUGGESTED READING

Finding Wounded Deer by John Trout Jr. (Woods N' Water Press, 2001)

This book is an exhaustive guide to tracking deer after they have been wounded. Diagnosing shots, understanding how an injured deer responds to threats and landscape features, and figuring out what to do when all else fails are covered in extraordinary depth. I reread Trout's book every year before the deer season starts.

Whitetail Advantage by David Samuel and Robert Zaiglin (Krause Publications, 2008)

Samuel and Zaiglin are both biologists who have brought together a wealth of information from the latest scientific research into deer behavior. Many old-time deer-hunting myths are shattered by the research presented by the authors. If you are interested in the finer points of whitetail behavior or intend to try your hand at trophy hunting, this is the book for you.

INDEX

Page numbers in *italics* indicate illustrations; number in **bold** indicate charts.

A

aged hindquarters, *butchering*, 149–51
aiming at deer, 110–14, 140
    basic positions, 112–14, *113*
    cardiopulmonary organs, 110
    nervous system, 110–12, *111*
anatomy/biology, whitetail deer, 26–36
    antlers, 33–35
    digestion, 27–30
    eyesight, *30*, 30–31
    hearing, 31–32
    pineal gland, 36
    smell, sense of, 32–33
antlers, 24, 25, 33–35, 104

B

baiting deer, 167
blacktails. *See* mule deer/blacktails
blood, tracking and, 125–27, *128*, 129
bow hunting, 84–89
bow types, 85–87
    compound, 86, *86*
    crossbow, 86–87, *87*
    recurve, 85, *86*
browse, 29
buck fever, 116, 117
bullets, 73–75
butchering, 141–53
    processing meat, 148–53
    quartering, 142–47
"button bucks," 21, *21*

C

cartridges, 63–73
    ballistic arc, *65*, **65**, 65–66
    common deer, 72
    cost/availability, 68–69
    high/moderately powered, 70
    how they work, *63*, 63–64, *64*
    large vs. small, 67–68
    low-powered, 71–72
    naming, 73
    recoil, 66–67
    rimfire and centerfire, 71
    specialty rounds, 69
    why choice matters, 64–66
cooking venison, 154–65
    Almost-butterflied Venison Parmesan, 159
    Bibimbap, 164
    Boboti, 161
    "gaminess," myth of, 155
    Sauerbraten, 163
    substitutions, 156
    Thyme and Butter Coiled Backstrap,
        160–161
    Venison and Sweet Potato Curry, 165
    Venison Chili, 162
    Venison Jerky, 158
    Venison Stroganoff, 157
cutting board/butcher's block, 149–50

D

death of deer, confirming, 131–32
digestion, details of, 27–30, *28*
dispersal, 23–24
dry-aging hindquarters, 148–49

E

eating patterns, 29
education, 10, 49
environmental changes, adapting to, 40–43
    competing species, decline in, 41
    food supply, increase in, 41
    human influence on environment, 41–42
    physical changes, 43
    population growth, 41
evolution of deer, 37–46
    antlers, development of, *38*, 38–40, *39*
    environmental changes, adapting to,
        40–43

F

fawning season, 17–20
field dressing, 133–38
  bringing deer home, 137
  cracking the sternum, 134–35
  incision, making, 134, *134*
  knives for, *132*, 133
  organs, removal of, *135*, 135–36, 137
finding deer, 97–104
  how they approach food, 99–100, *100*
  hunting during the rut, 103–4
  peak hunting times, 102–3
  positioning, 99
  steadying rifle, 100–101, *101*
  tree stands and, 98
  weather-related movements, 103
firearms, comparison of, 50–58
  handguns, 57–58
  muzzleloaders, *56*, 56–57
  rifles, 50–51, *51*
  shotguns, *51*, 52–56
following the trail, 127–29
  blood, 127–28, 129
  disturbed ground, 129
  parallel trails, 129
  shot types/tracking times, 128
follow-up shot, 121–23
  preparing for, 121
  when deer is down, 122
  when deer runs off, 123
food supply, increase in, 41
funneling deer traffic, *106*, 107

G

"gaminess," myth of, 155
gunsmithing screws/screwdrivers, 79, *79*
gutting, 139, 140. *See also* field dressing

H

handguns, 57–58
hunter education, 10, 49

K

knives, hunting/skinning, 132, *132*, 133

L

land use, hunting and, 166–71
  public land, 168–71
  small property, 105–7
  your backyard, 167–68
learning to hunt as an adult, 9–14
  first deer story, 13–14
  psychological preparation, 10–12
life cycles of deer/hunting seasons, **49**
linseed oil, wood treatment, 150
local regulations, 48–49

M

mule deer/blacktails, 43–46, *46*
muzzleloaders, *56*, 56–57

O

organs, removal of, *135*
  brain shot, and, 140
  colon, disconnection of, 135
  diaphragm, cutting the, 136–37
outsmarting deer, 93–97
  silence, as essential, 92–93
  staying downwind/scent control, 93–96,
    94, 97
  visual distractions and, 96
  white and blue, avoiding, 96–97

P

packaging meat, 150–51
peak hunting times, 102–3
physical changes, environment and, 43
politics of hunting, 88–89
population of deer, 19, 41
positions, deer presentation, 112–14, *113*
processing the meat, 148–53
  forequarters, 153
  hindquarter, boning, *152*, 152–53
  hindquarters, butchering aged, 149–51
  hindquarters, dry-aging, 148–49
  rind removal, 157, *157*
  scraps, collecting, 153
psychological preparation for hunting,
  10–12
public land, 168–71

Q

quartering, 142–47
  backstraps, removing, *145*, 145–46
  in the field, 139–40
  forequarters, removing, 144–45
  laying or hanging deer, 143
  less-desirable pieces, 147
  sharpening knife, 142
  skinning deer, *143*, 143–44
  tarsal glands, covering, 143
  tenderloin, removing, 146

R

rattling, 104
reasons to hunt, 6–9
recipes. *See* cooking venison
regulations, local, 48 49
rifles, 50–51, *51*, 58–62
  action types, 58–59, *59*
  bolt action, 60
  fitting of, 62
  lever action, 60
  semiautomatic, 61
  steadying, 100–101, *101*
  for women, 62
ruminating, basics, 27–29, *28*
rut, the, *21*, 21–22, 103–4

S

scope(s), 76–83
  attaching the sight, 80
  bore-sighting, 80–81, *81*
  cost and quality, 77–78
  installing, *79*, 79–83
  mounting/zeroing, 76, *76*
  premounted, 83
  rings/base for, 77, *77*
  zeroing, 82–83
scouting, 108, *108*
seasons/life cycles of deer, **49**
senses. *See under* anatomy/biology, white-
    tail deer
shooting
  fouling shot/clean barrel, 118
  moving deer, 119
  obstructed shot, 116, 118

  practice, 91–92
  unsteady hand and, 118–19
short-stroking, 115–16, *116*
shotguns, 52–56
  gauge and caliber, 55
  rifled slugs, 53
  sabot slugs, 54
  shotshells and, 52, *52*
  slug guns, 53
shot placement, 109–19
sighting apparatus, 76, *76*–78
  open sights, 76
  scopes, 76–78, *77*
socializing, spring, 20, *20*–21
springtime, *20*, 20–21, 25
supplies for hunting trip, 136

T

tracking, after the shot, 124–29
  behavior after the shot, 127
  blood, 125–27
  following the trail, 127–29, *128*
  hair, 124, *124*
  shot types/tracking times, 128
transporting gutted deer, 137

U

understanding deer, 15–25

V

venison. *See* cooking venison

W

weather-related movements, 103
where to hunt. *See* land use, hunting and
wilderness survival, 138
winter, 22–25, *24*

Y

year in life of deer, 17–25, *21*
  dispersal, 23–24
  fawning season, 17–20
  population control/malnutrition, 19
  rut, the, *21*, 21–22, 103–4
  springtime, *20*, 20–21, 25
  winter, 22–25, *24*

OTHER STOREY TITLES
YOU WILL ENJOY

THE BACKYARD LUMBERJACK, by Frank Philbrick & Stephen Philbrick.
Practical instruction and first-hand advice on the thrill of felling, bucking, splitting, and stacking wood.
176 pages. Paper. ISBN 978-1-58017-634-7.

THE BLACKSMITH'S CRAFT, by Charles McRaven.
Clear instructions and step-by-step photographs that show how to build a forge, make or acquire tools, and create items of lasting beauty.
256 pages. Paper. ISBN 978-1-58017-593-7.

COMPACT CABINS, by Gerald Rowan.
Simple living in 1,000 square feet or less — includes 62 design interpretations for every taste.
216 pages. Paper. ISBN 978-1-60342-462-2.

STOREY'S BASIC COUNTRY SKILLS, by John and Martha Storey.
A treasure chest of information on building, gardening, animal raising, and homesteading — perfect for anyone who wants to become more self-reliant.
576 pages. Paper. ISBN 978-1-58017-202-8.

TAN YOUR HIDE!, by Phyllis Hobson.
A step-by-step guide to making vests, belts, and wallets by home-tanning and hand-working furs and leathers.
144 pages. Paper. ISBN 978-0-88266-101-8.

WILD TURKEYS, by John J. Mettler Jr., DVM.
Complete habitat and mating information for hunting or observing these noble birds.
176 pages. Paper. ISBN 978-1-58017-069-7.

These and other books from Storey Publishing are available wherever quality books are sold or by calling 1-800-441-5700.
Visit us at *www.storey.com*.